STEADY LOVE

WHAT *Every* HEART LONGS FOR

A.R. GRIMMIE JR.

A JOURNEY OF FAITH, LOSS, AND HOPE

Steady Love

What Every Heart Longs For

A. R. Grimmie Jr.

Sevenhorns Publishing. New York, NY

Published by Sevenhorns Publishing, New York, NY

Cover art and *The Elvish Princess* by Cassie Wills

Library of Congress Control Number: 2026943942

ISBN

979-8-99608470-8 Hardcover

979-8-99608471-5 Paperback

979-8-99608472-2 Ebook

This book reflects the author's present recollections of lived experiences over time. Some names and identifying details have been changed to protect the privacy of others. Some events and conversations have been compressed or recreated for literary effect.

To my family:
Tina, Marcus, and Christina,
for displaying a love for one another that remained constant through life's highest joys and deepest sorrows.
Your unwavering love has been a gift, a witness, an inspiration, and a huge reason this book exists.
And to my mom, dad, and sister:
To my mom, who modeled love all the days of her life;
To my dad, for his devotion to his family;
and to my sister, for her faithful loving kindness.

Preface

The steadfast love of the Lord never ceases; his mercies never come to an end; they are new every morning; great is your faithfulness.

Lamentations 3:22, 23

Let me hear in the morning of your steadfast love, for in you I trust. Make me know the way I should go, for to you I lift up my soul.

Psalm 143:8

This book was born out of real life; shaped by love and laughter, sorrow and suffering, heartbreak and hope.

The stories in these pages are deeply personal, but their purpose reaches far beyond my own life or the life of my family. Two truths have followed me through every chapter of my life: God is real, and He created us for a relationship with Him.

These understandings did not come because I was inclined to believe without question. I have always been skeptical by nature, unwilling to accept anything as true simply because I was told it was so. I have wrestled deeply with the question of what is true. And through that very process, my confidence in the reality of God grew stronger. As I came to know His written Word more deeply, and as I saw the supernatural elements of His truth borne out in the events of my life, what I once examined from a distance became something I could no longer honestly deny. Again and again, Scripture and lived experience testified that God is not imagined, not invented, and not silent.

He has not left himself without witness. God the Father has revealed himself throughout history by the people He chose, through His written Word, and most fully through Jesus Christ, who entered our world, walked among us, and made him known.

The heart of the Christian faith is not merely that God exists, but that He has drawn near. He is neither distant, nor indifferent. He is the God who speaks, who enters into human suffering, and calls us into fellowship with himself. That truth has sustained me through seasons of joy and through valleys of death I never would have chosen. It has not answered every question, but it has given me Someone to trust who has beaten death itself.

Steady Love is not an attempt to explain every mystery of pain, loss, or providence. It is a testimony to the unwavering love, the loving loyalty of God in the middle of real life, where beauty and brokenness so often live side by side. I write with deep gratitude for the family, friends, and everyone whose love, prayers, encouragement, and faithfulness helped shape my life and these pages. In some places, minor details have been adjusted for clarity, privacy, or the flow of the narrative, but the heart of these accounts remains true to my recollection.

My prayer is that this book would do more than tell my family's story. I pray it would point beyond itself to the living God, who has made himself known and still invites men and women to come to him. If these pages stir even one heart to consider His reality, His nearness, and His steady love, then it will have served its deepest purpose.

A. R. Grimmie Jr.

Prologue

I pedaled my bike as fast as my legs could go down the twisty dirt road that went deep into the woods and farther from our house than any of us had ever been. I glanced back real quick to see how far behind my sisters, Loretta and Mae, were. It was 1935 and cars were as rare as a blue moon in West Berlin, the sleepy little town where we lived in New Jersey. My sisters always took their sweet time on the turns, but I just zoomed ahead.

The trees thinned on my right, and I spotted a little stream. I slowed up, and when the girls were within earshot, I yelled out to them. "Follow me!"

The tree line broke into a grassy field full of sunshine. I jumped off my bike and ran over to the water's edge. I grabbed some sticks and dug in the muddy ground.

I looked up, and there were Loretta and Mae, dropping their bikes by mine and half running, half skipping over to me.

"These are for you, slowpokes!" I yelled, laughing as I handed them each a stick. We kicked off our shoes and waded in the cool water, feeling the mud and grass squish between our toes. We dug little holes and watched them fill with water.

"I bet we're the only people who've ever been here," Mae said, lifting her face to the sun.

The sound of the splashing water and the sun sparkling on it made us feel like we were in a magical place. The dirt road was just beyond the trees, but here in the woods we felt like real explorers in a wild land.

A brick dam stuck out from where we were walking along the stream, and beyond that was a big pond where we could see frogs jumping in as we got closer.

I took the lead on our make-believe adventure, even though I was the youngest at seven. Loretta was nine, and Mae was ten, but since they were girls I got to be the captain. We lunged and swung our sticks, pretending to battle invisible bad guys.

Just when we were about to conquer the dam, I saw splashing farther out. I ran ahead and climbed onto the ledge, excited to get a closer look. "Ahhh! Tadpoles!"

"Be careful!" Loretta shouted, her voice all worried. "You know none of us can swim!"

"I know, I know," I shouted back. Loretta and Mae watched me with big eyes from the water's edge.

All I could think about were those tadpoles. I crawled on my hands and knees along the ledge to the end of the dam. I leaned way over, gasping with joy as I watched the tadpoles zip around in the water. They were so close, I was sure I could grab one. If I just leaned a little more—

Suddenly, I slipped right off the ledge and sank into the deep water below. I kicked my feet and flailed my arms, but it just pushed me away from the ledge and safety. My feet couldn't touch the bottom, and my head bobbed up and down while I gasped for air.

"Help!" I yelled, but all I got was a mouthful of water and started to choke. I tried to scream, but the words caught in my throat and the swirling pond swallowed me under again. I sank deeper this time, and the water felt colder around me. It had been so warm at the edge. I could hear my sisters screaming, but it sounded far away, like I was in a dream—

***

Are our lives just a scattered series of random events? Or is there a day coming, a moment of revelation, when everything will come into focus? When what once felt disconnected will suddenly make sense in the light of something far greater?

Could it be that something exists, so unfailing and unshakable, so powerful that even our deepest aches and longings are woven into its purpose? A guiding hand that not only brings meaning to the past, but awakens a kind of holy nostalgia for something we've glimpsed but not yet fully seen?

Even in a world as troubled as ours, is it possible that we can catch glimpses of that wonder right here, right now?

***

Just when everything started to go dark, I felt strong hands grab me and pull me out of the water.

Later, I found out that my sister had run through the field yelling for help just as a man driving one of the few cars around was passing by on that empty back road.

Albert R. Grimmie Sr.

My father, Albert Raymond Grimmie Sr. nearly drowned in a pond in the woods when he was seven years old. He shared this story with me and my sister many times while we were growing up, mostly whenever he and Mom took us to the Jersey shore beaches or to swim in my aunt's pool. Dad never swam. The fear of water stayed with him all of his life after that day on the dam in 1935. Even so, the unlikelihood of anyone driving along that empty back road at the exact moment his life was in danger was not lost on my dad. To him, this wasn't just a childhood memory. It was a miracle.

It wasn't until I was in high school and got my driver's license that I found that very road, along with the stream and the pond where my dad's life had been spared some forty years earlier. It was still a back road with little traffic.

I wondered if it really had been a miracle that my dad was saved that day, or was it just chance? Either way, I would not be here if he had drowned. So, am I here by chance, or by a God-ordained miracle?

Chapter One

The End

I leaned over and wrapped my arms around my wife, Tina, as best I could. I rested my head beside hers on the pillow, cheek to cheek like we'd done for thirty-one years. But this time, instead of her waking and our eyes meeting, I knew she'd breathed her final breath as Jesus carried her home.

The room was quiet except for the soft rushing of nurses around her bedside. I stood by, watching, facing my own helplessness. Twenty-three years of the constant commotion of living with breast cancer, endless doctor visits, alternative treatments that offered hope but faded was over. Tina had been a trooper through it all. Most of the time if you saw her in the middle of the day, you'd never know anything was wrong with her. Only our family knew that she'd start slow in the morning, be full of life during the day, and fold up early at night. Over the years that window kept getting smaller and smaller. Silently, it had closed.

I saw more than heard the sound as the doctor's lips formed the words to say what I already knew. *"She's gone."*

The drive home afterward felt endless, a hollow road stretching out beneath me, carrying me away from the love and life I once knew.

In the days following that September 2nd morning in 2018, I drifted between numbness and obligation. Friends suggested that I cancel the fundraising event planned for the 25th, but my son Marcus and I both knew what Tina would have wanted us to do: push forward.

Left: Albert "Bud" Jr. and Tina on their wedding day

Bud and Tina

Working through the Christina Grimmie Foundation had been therapeutic for our family. Before Tina died, in the eighteen months after Christina was killed, we served everywhere we could. We were on a mission to offer a real pathway to hope through financial and emotional support for shooting victims and their families. We poured our hearts into helping people whose lives were torn apart by a pain we knew all too well.

The night of the fundraising event, carrying on without Tina, I felt as though I were wading through mud. My body was present, but my spirit was far away. Almost too weary to feel God's nearness, I made it through the presentation, often feeling like I was at a loss for words that nevertheless kept coming. In the quiet aching of my battered heart, I sensed myself being carried along on familiar rhythms; but I felt more like footprints being blown away in the sand than someone being held by God. I breathed a long, shaky sigh of relief when the event was over. Driving away from Los Angeles that night, I felt like a shadow of myself, emptied, alone, unsure of how to face the next day.

October sped by in a blur of going through the motions. Meetings at the Foundation's command central–our dining room–with our small team of my son

Marcus and good friends Sue Procko and Tony Scott answering emails and going on with the business of running the Foundation. Most days I felt overwhelmed, a tide of emotion crashing over me in wave after relentless wave. The second anniversary of my daughter Christina's death had been just a few months earlier on June 10th, and the shadow of losing Tina on September 2nd still hung heavy.

I opened another email and pushed through the ache in my heart. The age-old question of how a good God could let this happen kept eating at me. Yet, I couldn't help but remember how cancer had ravaged Tina's body, but never her spirit.

Back in May, Tina's oncologist at UCLA had given us hospice papers.

"The cancer will take you," he said.

Quick as a whip, Tina corrected him. "My Lord and Savior will take me when He is good and ready."

And just four short months later, on September 2nd, my Boo, my beloved Tina, was gone. I hoped helping others who had suffered tragic loss would fill the void she left behind.

Then, as if the world itself mirrored my brokenness, on November 7th, a mass shooting at the Borderline Bar and Grill shook our community in Thousand Oaks. Twelve people were shot dead, and many more were wounded. The very next day, raging fires forced Marcus and me to evacuate our home.

We got busy doing all we could, reaching out through the Foundation and connecting with the County Victim Service to help. We wanted to be there for people, to offer a pathway to hope in the wake of the shootings. It felt good to serve others, but I couldn't shake the weariness I felt gnawing at me. If I were to continue this work, I knew I needed to slow down, to breathe.

It was in this swirl of tragedy and disorientation that Tony placed an early Christmas gift in my hands: *The 100-Day Goal Journal - Accomplish What Matters.* At the time, I thought it a strange gift to give a man whose heart was shattered. I had no idea what mattered most to me now. Yet that journal became a small reminder that I was still here, still moving, still searching for how to move forward, or at times, how not to utterly collapse.

Tina Marie Grimmie

When my father was seven years old, he nearly drowned. One moment he was flailing in the water, and the next, strong hands pulled him out and onto dry land. That brush with death became one of the defining moments of his childhood, a story of being saved when all seemed lost. It was only years later that I began to understand how moments like that, where life and death hang in the balance, can shape the way we see God's hand at work, even when we don't fully recognize it in the moment.

As I flipped through the pages of the journal, I thought about my father being saved and Tina and Christina both being gone. In that collision of memory and loss, all I knew was that I needed solitude. I needed time alone with my thoughts and with God. I wondered if He'd still be there for me, without Tina. I needed space to let the numbness sink in, to wrestle with the silence of God, and to search for what Tina and I had experienced many times in our thirty-one years of marriage. She called it, "a God thing," or a divine encounter. Would I ever feel God's love again through this apathy? I remembered bible verses about God's love for me. I needed Him now more than ever in the face of everything that had changed. I had suffered one tragic, traumatic loss in an instant, and a second that was twenty-three years in the making.

Mercifully, some empty blocks had appeared on my calendar at the end of the year. I was heading home to New Jersey for Christmas and New Year's, hoping two weeks in the familiarity of home would help me reclaim the peace of mind I so desperately needed.

Chapter Two

Beginnings

Marcus maneuvered through the traffic on the 405, threading our way south to the airport. In L.A., they say that someone truly loves you if they're willing to drive you to LAX. As we crept along, even the radiant Southern California sunshine felt dimmed by the clouds that hung over my spirit.

Staring out the window, my mind drifted back to the whirlwind of events that led us from New Jersey to California. The years had slid by like cars racing on the L.A. freeways, some moments a blur of joy, others grinding to a halt in agonizing gridlock.

***

"Do you think this guy can help us?" Tina asked, her voice cut through the stillness as we sat trapped in bumper-to-bumper traffic on the 101. We were on our way to meet Mike Frost, the vice president of the Communications Workers of America (CWA) union at Verizon. I'd spoken to Mike over the past few months about transferring out west to be with my family. Tina and Christina were already living in L.A., nurturing Christina's blossoming music career while I remained in New Jersey, tethered to my job in communications at Verizon. Marcus, our son, would be moving to California in September to attend Musicians Institute in Hollywood.

Left: A walk on the beach at dawn

During our conversations, Mike shared how his daughter was a big fan of Christina's. We'd sent her a t-shirt and some merch, and Christina called her on her birthday. Mike had been so appreciative. It warmed my heart to know that such a simple gesture had left such an impression on him. After that, I decided that during my next visit with Tina and Christina in L.A. I would make an appointment to meet Mike in person.

"I'm not sure. And I'm a little nervous," I replied, taking my eyes off the traffic for a second to glance at Tina. "But I can't bear the thought of another year living apart."

I believed God would make the path clear when the time was right for me to join Tina and the kids in L.A. Deep in my spirit, I sensed God saying, "Pay attention. Stay close. Stay prayerful." That feeling seriously heightened my awareness. For more than a year I went to two church services on Sundays and men's Bible study on Saturday morning at FAC and Wednesday nights at Calvary Chapel in Marlton. I had also been reading and praying with other men, desperate to keep my eyes open and not miss whatever door God opened for me to move. More than wanting a door to open, we wanted the wisdom to know when it was truly his. But nothing had happened yet. I hoped meeting with Mike would change that.

When we finally arrived at his office in Burbank, I introduced Mike to Tina, and we chatted while we waited for his secretary, Kate, who was stuck in traffic.

While we waited, T Santora, the president of the CWA union workers walked into Mike's office. He immediately said to Mike, "So, this is the guy you've been telling me about?" He sounded politely curious.

"Yes," Mike said, nodding. "Al has almost twenty-five years with Verizon."

"And what do you do at Verizon, Al?" he asked, turning to face me directly.

"I'm a splicer," I replied, my voice steady despite the storm of emotions beginning to swirl inside me. "I've spent 15 years splicing copper, and now I'm a fiber-optic splicer—"

His eyebrows shot up, and his eyes widened with surprise. "Did you know AT&T is actively looking for splicers in L.A. who are proficient in both?"

Tina and I exchanged a glance, a spark of hope igniting in our hearts. Dare we dream?

"How would that work?" I asked. "Would I need to quit Verizon, or transfer?"

"We can work out the details," T assured me. "How close are you to retiring?"

"I'll be eligible on March 30th, my 55th birthday," I replied. It was January of 2013.

"They're hiring April 1st!" T Santora said.

Tina and I looked at each other again. Could God be making it clear?

In that moment, the weight of our dreams felt tangible, almost within reach. It turned out that on my birthday, March 30th, I would hit the right age and years of service to retire from Verizon in New Jersey and seamlessly transition to AT&T in California on April 1st. I might not even miss a day of work. Suddenly, being reunited with my family felt possible—even probable.

Tina and I hardly noticed the traffic on the 101 heading back to our rented apartment in Sherman Oaks. We could hardly believe what had just happened.

Just as we stepped inside our apartment, my phone rang, jolting us back from dreams of finally living together as a family again. It was my union rep back home, his voice urgent. "Hey, Al, I know you're on vacation, but I have to let everyone in our garage know— Verizon is offering a double Incentive Separation Package as an enticement for early retirement. You just have to decide by April 1st."

In that moment, clarity struck like lightning. God couldn't have made it any clearer—it was time for me to join my family in California.

***

"Dad," Marcus' voice pulled me from my thoughts, grounding me in the present, where hope and heartache intertwined. "We're here."

He pulled in behind a long line of cars double-parked curbside in front of the American Airlines terminal. He jabbed the red triangle in the middle of the dashboard, and the car's hazard lights blinked on. Instead of hopping out and running around to where I was about to get out on the passenger side, Marcus sat back in the driver's seat and looked directly into my eyes.

"Is this the first time you've taken this flight without Mom?" His question hung in the air until finally, I nodded.

"Yep," I said.

We sat for a moment. Then Marcus came around to the passenger side and opened the door to help with my bag. We hugged for a long time and said our goodbyes. I promised to text when I landed. I waved as he drove off, then headed into a bustling LAX.

I thought about Marcus' question as I moved through TSA Pre-check. I'd never taken this flight without Tina. It felt surreal to be doing it now.

When we were first married, before we'd ever heard the word "cancer," before the tests, before the scans, before the chemotherapy, Tina and I traveled often. Sometimes we'd just head off on a whim for road trips and weekend getaways filled with long talks in hotel lobbies and coffee shops. We explored new places and learned how to navigate life together, not just on the road, but in the deeper, sacred spaces of marriage.

Silently, I joined the hundreds, maybe thousands of people milling about, talking, laughing, scrolling—doing the work of getting through the airport. Absent from the noise was the sound of my wife's voice. The early years of our marriage were some of the sweetest, most formative years of our lives, filled with conversations about faith, family, communication, forgiveness, and joy. We'd had space and time to simply be together, to explore new places and grow not just as husband and wife, but as best friends, fellow seekers, and co-laborers in faith.

I drifted through the routine of getting through the airport, glad I didn't have to go through the hassle of taking off my shoes or dropping them in bins. I watched as people sent their stuff along into the black hole in the middle of the conveyor belt.

"Sir, is this your bag? Are those your shoes?" The TSA attendant directed her questions to someone in line. Her voice broke into my thoughts.

I grabbed my backpack as it slid out from the scanner and headed for my gate.

I always liked getting to the airport super early. For the two hours prior to boarding I mentally navigated the trip ahead, my heart longing to find solid ground—even if it only existed in my past.

The hum of voices and the shuffle of hurried footsteps surrounded me in the cavernous halls of LAX, but I felt strangely detached. Travelers rushed along, rolling bags, checking phones, chasing connections, yet I moved at my own pace, slow and deliberate. My mind had long left Los Angeles, anticipating my return to my childhood home. I wasn't headed east just to visit. I was chasing something more elusive: solitude—a place where I could think, grieve, and listen without interruption.

I kept walking, driven by an inward pull, until I reached my gate. Dropping into a seat, I found my flight on the digital board. More than two hours before boarding. Perfect. Two solid hours to wait. Two solid hours for memories to stir. I felt the tug of New Jersey before I ever stepped onto the plane—childhood streets, young love, triumphs, regrets, the laughter and tears of family life. I looked forward to walking on the beach at Ocean City where I'd proposed to Tina, and leaning on the fence at the soccer field where we first met. I planned to sit outside the apartment in Voorhees where we'd shared our first kiss, and in Sicklerville, where we lived when our kids were born. I imagined Mom and Dad's house on Franklin Avenue where I grew up in Berlin, and the old Edgewood High School, where I'd spent so many hours playing basketball. I'd drive by Garden Lake Bible Church, where I first attended men's bible study. My past rose up like a tide I couldn't stop, and I welcomed it.

I sat at my gate, watching the minutes crawl. I needed this space of waiting. In this forced pause, the threads of my life story knotted and re-knotted in my mind. How would I begin to grapple with the tangle of emotions inside me—unresolved questions, half-buried grief, the ache of both loss and love? In the crowd of strangers, I felt completely alone. And without Tina, that aloneness, for the first time in a long while, was exactly what I wanted.

Chapter Three

What Every Heart Longs For

I looked around at the usual lineup of coffee shops and gift kiosks, their bright lights and canned music a sharp contrast to the heaviness pressing on my chest. How cheerful they'd seemed with Tina by my side. Thinking of traveling in those early days with her sent a pang of longing through my heart, but what I treasured most from that time wasn't the trips or the scenery. It was just being with Tina. Our love seemed to deepen as we shared our faith and simply enjoyed being together. We were lost in the wonder of discovering a kindred spirit.

We prayed and read Scripture together. We would end up in long, honest conversations, sometimes late into the night, about things we read in the Bible about suffering, hope, and what it meant to trust God with our lives. In those years, we weren't just building a marriage, we were laying a foundation of a faith that would carry us through every storm to come. A faith not rooted in feelings or formulas, but in God's word, in relationship, in love, both God's for us and ours for each other. I would often end our prayer time together with the words, *"... and I ask that Tina and I would grow closer together as we grow closer to You."*

We didn't know then what lay ahead. We didn't know that a mammogram would lead to a biopsy, and the biopsy would lead to words no one ever wants to hear—

Left: Tina and her parents, Skip and Gina

"Ladies and gentlemen, we'll now begin boarding American Airlines flight 2832 from Los Angeles to Philadelphia..." The voice of reality broke into my thoughts. Suddenly the two hours were gone. Once onboard, I tucked my backpack beneath the seat in front of me and settled in for the five-hour flight. Out on the tarmac, baggage attendants in orange and yellow safety vests zipped around on golf carts between planes loading passengers and preparing for takeoff.

Early on, Tina and I had no idea where our journey would take us. We didn't know what was coming or how much our lives would change.

But God knew. And I believe He gave us those times of joy and fullness, not as a tease before the storm, but as an anchor through it. He gave us those memories to hold onto.

"... Please remain in your seats with your seatbelts fastened while the "Fasten Seatbelt" sign is on. There's weather ahead, and we're anticipating light turbulence–"

The early years were great, but not without real problems that threatened to derail our relationship. Over the years we grew spiritually while raising kids, living with cancer, dealing with finances, and navigating lots of experiences couples go through. Later, when we led bible study for young married couples, we'd share how we'd learned to overcome senseless arguments, pushing through tough times together and not giving up on our marriage.

Inevitably, someone would ask the question—

"How long have you two been married?"

"It's been about 15 years, right?" I'd look at Tina for confirmation.

"Yes, 15 years," she'd say.

"Yep, it's been 14 of the best years of my life," I'd say, and everyone would look at us, confused.

"That first year was a bear!" I'd say.

Tina would playfully hit me, saying, *"Seriously, I don't know how he stayed with me that first year. I was a bear."*

And that little interchange, along with Tina's transparency, would always make the couples feel more at ease talking about their own struggles. I remember like it was yesterday, Tina sharing how the first year of our marriage had been so turbulent—how her past had made it so difficult for her to trust me as her husband. Her dad had cheated on her mother. Her uncle cheated on her aunt.

Boyfriends had been unfaithful to her instead of returning the love she was so willing to give.

That first year we were married Tina wanted to trust me, but she just didn't. She worried that I would be unfaithful. And she kept pushing me away because one voice in her head was telling her she was not good enough, that I would give up on her, while another voice tried to convince her that the true love she longed for was possible. Together, we struggled to trust God to help heal the hurt and distrust cemented in her past.

Tina grew up on Clearview Avenue in Pine Hill, a small town in New Jersey. As a young girl, she adored her parents, but her father, Wesley "Skip" Milos held a special place in her heart. Skip's parents were Romanian immigrants whose marriage had been arranged back in their homeland. Skip had an air of strength and charisma that Tina idolized. Her mother, Gina Carretti, came from a vibrant Italian family, making Tina a fiery combination of both heritages.

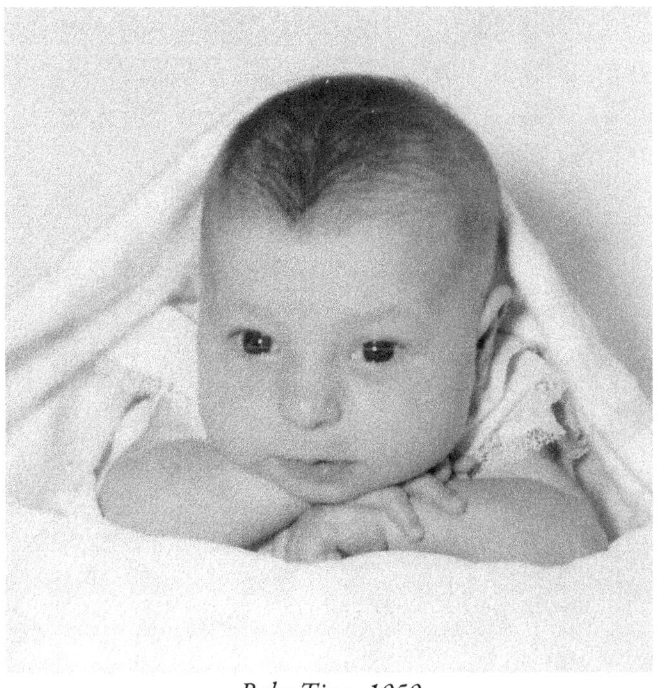

Baby Tina, 1959

When she was eight years old, Tina's parents—eager for free childcare—dropped her off at a local Vacation Bible School. Tina loved the songs and crafts, and it was there at VBS that she first heard about God's perfect love. The simple yet profound message that Jesus loved her deeply and unconditionally stayed with her. The idea that believing in His sacrifice could guarantee a place with God forever captivated her. It was a stark contrast to the chaos always brewing at home.

Skip's mother, Mary Milos lived across the street for a few years, and though she worked long hours she always made time for Tina. As time went on and the cracks in her parents' relationship widened, Grandmom Milos' love would become a safe haven in Tina's life. She had raised two sons—Tina's dad Skip and her uncle Gary—but she doted on Tina and showered her with the affection she longed to show a daughter of her own.

Grandmom Milos, sons Gary and Wesley (Skip)

By the time she was a teenager, Tina routinely overheard arguments that escalated into full-blown fights, mostly over finances. Her mother worked at the local Acme Market, obsessing over money and making ends meet. Gina was distant, often criticizing Tina, leaving her feeling she could never measure up. And her father's love, once a source of comfort, began to feel shallow.

Tina faced health challenges as a teen—including a diagnosis of endometriosis requiring her to undergo a painful surgery and the devastating prognosis that she might never have children. Skip's refrain of, *"I love you, 'Teen, but I can't help you right now,"* only deepened her sense of isolation. Tina told herself she didn't want kids, anyway.

Tina adored her father, Skip and kept his secrets

During her parents' fights her mother's sharp voice would cut through the air. Her father would eventually just grab his keys and leave. Tina found their fights confusing and unsettling. Caught up in their clashes, she clung to her father, her childhood hero. She sided with him against her mother's fierce anger.

Skip rewarded Tina's devotion and trust with lies. One afternoon she came home from school early and found him in *her* bed with another woman. The sight shattered her. Her idol, the man she believed could do no wrong became the source of her deepest pain. Tina lashed out furiously at Skip, but he persuaded her to keep the affair a secret from her mother. That decision weighed heavily on Tina and compounded her anger and heartbreak. The lie firmly planted ugly seeds that would blossom into suspicion and distrust in her relationships. The man she had once trusted above all else had betrayed her mother and made her complicit in his lying and cheating.

I was jolted awake as the plane lurched to the left, and the sounds of passengers gasping in surprise and fear filled the cabin. The "Fasten Seatbelt" signs glowed red from one end of the aisle to the other.

"Ladies and gentlemen, please return to your seats and fasten your seatbelts until we've cleared the weather and the captain turns off the "Fasten Seatbelt" sign. We apologize for the delay, but snack and beverage service will begin at that time."

I covered my eyes with my hands and massaged both temples with my thumbs. The glorified tin can we flew in bumped along over swells and pockets of air 35,000 feet above the ground.

How fragile life is. Her father's betrayal and the constant tension at home buffeted Tina's mental and physical health. She developed stress hives and began smoking heavily in her teens to cope. Tina hid her struggles well, but inside she grappled with depression and a deep sense of loss. Her childhood dream of finding true love—kind, patient, and unwavering like the one she'd heard about in vacation Bible school seemed unattainable.

Yet, even in the darkest moments, the seeds of unconditional love planted in her childhood at VBS and by Grandmom Milos remained buried in her heart, fighting to overcome her doubts. Back then Tina's journey was far from over, but her struggles were making her stronger. One day she'd discover that love, hope, and redemption were within reach after all.

I sighed and pulled my hoodie tighter around my shoulders. Suddenly, the flight seemed long, the memories stop feeling like a story I'm recalling and start feeling like a weight I'm carrying in real time. I remember reading in GriefShare that the pain of our grief is directly proportional to our love for the one we lose. The numb, dazed feeling is gone. My pain and loss is staggeringly real.

Tina, my life partner, my best friend—gone, and it hadn't even been four months. Christina, my precious, 22-year-old daughter, taken in a moment that still doesn't make sense. Two-and-a-half years later the shock still lived in my body like it was yesterday. One loss, sudden and traumatic; the other twenty-three years in the making. And now, they sit together inside me, side by side, demanding to be felt. I wanted to cry out to God as loudly as my heart was beating, but on a plane, surrounded by strangers, I was held in place by a seatbelt and etiquette. I swallowed the sound and let the grief escape through tears flooding my eyes, relentless, blurring the aisle and everything around me. I stare forward like I'm fine, blinking hard, breathing shallow. The ache keeps rising, anyway; a desperate lament, caught in my throat.

Lord, I don't know how to carry this. I don't know how to live in a world where they're not here.

"Would you like something to drink, sir?" The flight attendant's question jolted me back to reality.

I was looking forward to two solid weeks of being alone in Ocean City. It would be a ghost town in winter.

Chapter Four

The Beach in December

"*Are you sure you want to be staying on the beach in December?"* Marcus had asked when I told him I planned to spend the last two weeks of the year in Ocean City. He asked as though he thought it was a bad idea.

But there was no doubt in my mind, I knew exactly where I needed to be. As soon as my flight landed and I'd picked up a rental car I headed straight for Ocean City. The beach there had been mine and Tina's special place. While we were dating, Tina and I talked of marriage often, and way back when, I'd had my heart set on asking her to marry me there.

From the start, we were very clear in our intentions. We shared a lot of laughs and a lot of dreams—some whispered, some bold. One of our favorite pastimes was strolling through malls, casually window shopping for rings we couldn't yet afford. One evening, we ended up at Gordon's Jewelers in the Deptford Mall, and Tina saw the ring. I already knew her well enough to know that she had fallen in love with it. I can still see the way her eyes lit up.

I tried to play it down. *"Somehow, someday, I'll get that kind of money,"* I told her, *"because I love you—and I do want to marry you."*

She heard the promise, but what stuck with her most was the "someday." After that, signs spelling out "W-H-E-N" with a big question mark began to appear.

Left: Ocean City beach at sunset, winter 2018

The first one showed up in the apartment she shared with her mom at the time. I went to pick Tina up after work one day, and there it was, taped up on the wall in all its handmade glory. I couldn't help but laugh. Tina wasn't waiting quietly—she was counting on me, and she made sure I didn't forget it.

A few days later, I visited her at work—she was a receptionist at a mortgage company—and sure enough, another "WHEN?" sign hung near her desk. Tina had a way of making her point with charm and a little mischief.

Eventually, I'd saved enough for a down payment and a plan. I returned to Gordon's, gave them the deposit, got approved for the rest, and took the ring home. I told my parents I was going to propose. I could hardly wait to propose to Tina at the beach in Ocean City—our special place.

Soon after, I called Tina at work one afternoon. I noticed she sounded congested. She told me her allergies were flaring up. *"Let's go to the shore when you get off,"* I said, seizing the opportunity. *"The ocean air always helps you breathe better."* She agreed without hesitation.

I picked her up right after work, and we headed for Ocean City. Her dad lived near 28th Street, so we parked nearby and walked through the dunes until we reached the shoreline. The sun was low, the breeze soft, and our hands were entwined as we walked north along the water's edge, making small talk.

Later, Tina told me that during that walk, she started to worry. *"He brought me out here to break up with me,"* she thought.

But the truth was, I had never been more certain.

I stopped, let go of her hand, looked her in the eyes, and knelt in the sand.

"Tina, will you marry me?"

Before I could even finish pulling the ring out of my pocket, she was already saying, *"Yes! Yes! I will marry you!"*

As soon as I handed her the ring, she took off, darting into the ocean up to her knees. I laughed out loud, but prayed silently, *"Please don't drop the ring, T!"*

Later she confessed, *"You started to kneel, and I was like—he better have a ring!"*

***

I was lost in thought as the car practically drove itself along the Atlantic City Expressway. I'd traveled that road so many times with Tina. I took the exit for Ocean City and made my way past the condo where her dad had moved with his new wife after he'd divorced Tina's mom. I crossed over to 28th Street. I parked in what seemed like the exact same spot Tina and I had some thirty-one years ago, but tonight I sat alone in the rental car.

After a while, I braved the cold and got out of the car. Desperate to feel some connection with Tina, I crossed the street and threaded my way through the dunes to the deserted beach. The crashing of the green-gray waves against the sand matched my mood, and yet, the familiarity of the place was comforting to me. Looking back, that moment on the beach was more than just a marriage proposal. It was a snapshot of the love Tina and I shared—joyful, playful, committed, and deeply rooted in trust. Tina didn't just wait for love—she believed in it. She held me accountable to the promises I made, not with pressure, but with lighthearted confidence that love was worth expecting. I longed for that confidence now.

I stood in the cold, watching the ocean and let memories of lighter days wash over me in endless waves. When the sun started to dip below the horizon, I decided it was time to head over to the condo I'd rented. The short drive from the beach took me, again, past Tina's dad's condo. Tina had confided in me until her memories felt like my own, and the thought of the pain he'd caused her sent a ripple of fresh anger through me. For a moment I readily traded my grief for that anger.

***

Tina's senior year of high school was anything but a time of celebration. Once, her house had been a refuge, and her room had been her sanctuary. Now, those same walls seemed to close in on her, haunting her with memories she couldn't escape.

The image of her father—a man she'd once idolized—in her bed with another woman lingered in her mind, a cruel betrayal that had shattered the foundation of her world.

For years Tina carried the weight of his secret alone, the shame and disgust gnawing at her daily. She saw just two ways to escape: get married and leave, or end her life. Marriage seemed the better choice, and her boyfriend, Billy, was kind enough. But he wasn't the man of her dreams, and Tina knew deep down that love didn't lie down that path. And the more she contemplated marrying Billy the more depressed she became.

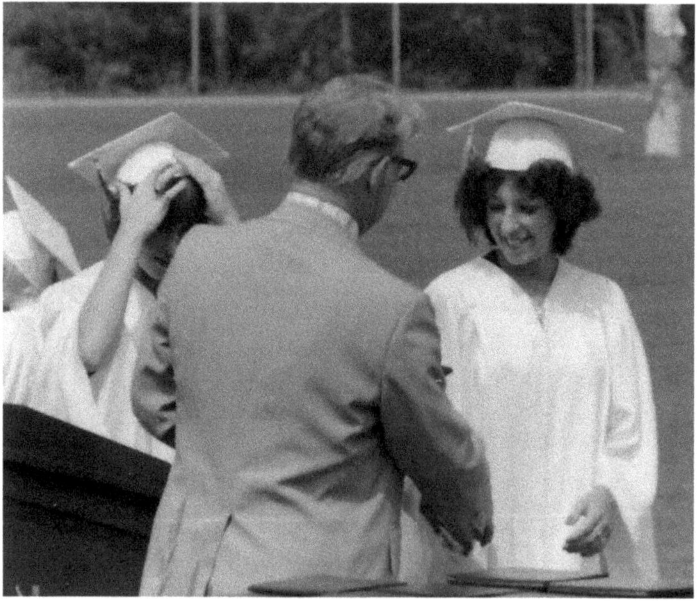

Tina's high school graduation

One day, after another long and lonely walk through an empty house, Tina sought relief in the liquor cabinet. She took a sip of whiskey that burned her throat, then mixed it with whatever else she found, hoping to numb the ache inside. For a brief moment, the storm quieted, but despair quickly returned. Her thoughts turned darker, and emboldened by the alcohol, she decided it was time to end her pain. She found a bottle of prescription pills in her parents' medicine cabinet and swallowed them, one after another, until the bottle was empty.

But instead of relief, she felt her stomach churn and her head spin. She stumbled into the bathroom, turned on the shower and stepped in, fully clothed, hoping the cold water might stop the overwhelming feeling of sickness. The last thing she remembered was the sound of the water cascading over her.

When her mother Gina came home, she found Tina unconscious, drenched and helpless at the bottom of the shower. Panicked, she rushed Tina to the hospital, where doctors pumped her stomach. She survived, but the emotional wounds she carried deepened.

The next day, Tina lay in her darkened room, shades drawn, feeling the weight of it all and trying to block out the sound of her parents arguing with each other and Grandmom Milos. In their shouting, she caught a shocking revelation.

"I never wanted her in the first place!" Gina shrieked. The secret, now spoken aloud, pierced Tina's already wounded heart. Her mother had tried to abort her before she was born. The betrayal struck Tina like lightning, compounding the hurt inflicted by her father's infidelity.

The house she had grown up in, once a place of security, now suffocated her. Tina did what she had learned to do—she hid her pain behind a can-do attitude and pushed forward. She graduated from high school, but instead of hope, she felt trapped. She took a job at a security company answering phones and managing the switchboard, pouring herself into her work and finding solace in the independence of earning her own money.

Sometimes, after work she'd stop at Fuddrucker's, a local bar and grill that was a big hit in the community. There, a few drinks helped her escape the pain of her fractured family. The alcohol dulled the ache, but the sense of emptiness remained. Now, marrying Billy seemed like her only way out. The two of them began planning a wedding, not out of love, but out of Tina's necessity.

On their wedding night, sitting together in Billy's small apartment, the truth they had been avoiding came to light. They both knew they had made a mistake. After just a few days, Tina confided in her parents, hoping for their support and help in undoing the marriage, but they refused to let her return home. Instead, they told her to honor her decision, especially since they'd spent so much money on the wedding.

So, with her belongings packed into the blue 1977 Cadillac Coupe DeVille her dad had given her and her loyal German shepherd, Tippy by her side, Tina left Billy's apartment. She drove around aimlessly, tears streaming down her face, desperate and unsure of what to do next.

She thought of God for the first time in years. Were the vacation bible school promises just cute children's stories, fairytales that would never come true for her—or were they truth? *Did God care about her? Was He even there?*

Tina and Tippy

Three decades later, losing my beloved wife and daughter had me asking the same questions. I had come to this crossroad a few times over the years. Looking back, each time I had chosen to keep pursuing God, to keep learning about Him and living according to His will as best I understood it. Tina and I had tried to live good Christian lives. But now, I wondered how I would go on. I wasn't sure I wanted to continue following God if I was going to suffer so much pain and sorrow anyway. The thought was oddly liberating. Suddenly, I felt free to choose my own way, to chart my own path.

Chapter Five

Bad Choices

I pulled the car back onto the street and drove past the condo where Tina's dad lived before he died of prostate cancer. I thought about my own dad and how different they were. Skip had blown up Tina's life, making her keep a secret that made it hard for her to trust that anyone truly loved her, even God. My dad had done the opposite. His love for my mother was steady, visible. Watching him had never pushed me away from God; it had quietly given me space to decide for myself whether love like that could be real.

I grew up attending Episcopal church services with my parents and my sister Carole every Sunday. My parents made me go. But one sunny afternoon as I was standing in my bedroom about to close the door, my dad walked in with news that would change the course of my life. His words marked a crossroad I would come to many times over the years.

"Bud," he began, (my family and friends have called me "Bud" since I was a kid. My dad was called Bud, too.) *"I want you to know, now that you're seventeen and have your own car, you don't have to ride to church with us on Sundays anymore. You can drive yourself. And, as a matter of fact," he continued, "you're old enough to decide whether you want to go at all. It should be your choice."*

I paused for a moment, letting his words sink in. Then I replied, "Well, that's great, Dad. Thanks."

And with that, he left the room.

Left: Albert "Bud" Sr. and Caroline on their wedding day

Bud and his sister, Carole

I remember the sound of my aunt Nancy and Uncle Paul chatting with my mom in the living room, their voices mingling with the easy hum of a lazy afternoon. But what sticks with me most–probably because of the significance of my dad's words–is the overwhelming feeling of freedom that washed over me. I thought he'd given me great news. No more boring church services! I could finally have my Sundays to myself!

Over the next few months I may have gone to church once or twice, but each time only confirmed what I already felt. Church just wasn't for me. It was dull, predictable. The music left much to be desired, and the constant rituals of standing, sitting, and kneeling irritated rather than inspired me. Nothing seemed to reach me or stir anything in me. I decided Sundays were better spent elsewhere.

At seventeen, the choice felt easy. I was free to chart my own path, and that's exactly what I did–without much thought for where that path might eventually lead. It felt good to make a decision for myself. I knew nothing about the consequences of bad choices or how one wrong move could change my life and lead to more bad choices. But back then I was about to start the learning process the hard way.

I spent the summer playing basketball and hanging out with my friends. I did my share and more of smoking pot, getting involved with too many girls, and making one bad choice after another. I was always the kid who was goaded into doing something reckless, the goodie two-shoes my friends liked to push to see how far I'd go to fit in. Now that I was free to spend my time as I pleased, they didn't have to push too hard.

I was in high school, and my dad had bought me my first car–an old Corvair that he lovingly restored. It was a piece of junk when he got it, but he had it painted, put new carpet on the floor and everything–to give to me. And it was a fast car. It had four carburetors, and the engine was in the back. It was also dangerous to drive, but my dad and I didn't know that at the time.

My friend Burley had a '74 Duster, and I had my Corvair. We loved to cruise side-by-side up and down Route 73, which ran right past the old Edgewood High School and eventually connected with the Atlantic City Expressway. We'd get to the long stretch of the road where there were no interruptions and start pushing the limits of our cars, going faster and faster. One particular afternoon, I remember hitting a hundred miles an hour. I'll never forget glancing over, seeing Burley matching my pace, our engines roaring, both of us flying down Route '73.

Then, looking back at the road, I spotted a truck up ahead in my lane. It couldn't have been going more than thirty-five miles an hour. I did some quick mental math—at a hundred miles an hour I'd hit him in no time. For a split second I considered slamming on the brakes to slow down and go around him. But I knew I'd have to drop behind Burley. I didn't want to lose. My pride, and maybe even a little stupidity kicked in. I had to make a choice, and fast. I jammed the pedal to the floor as hard as I could. The car shook all around me, straining with the effort. But I was inching ahead of Burley. I thought, *"I can do this if I keep the pedal down."*

With my heart pounding and no room to spare, I yanked the wheel and cut over in front of Burley. I was sure I hadn't gotten far enough past him. *"I'm going to hit him,"* I thought, bracing for the impact.

Then, the truck whooshed by; everything seemed to go dead quiet. I don't even remember the drive back to the school parking lot. But when Burley and I got out of our cars, we were both shaking.

"Did that really just happen?" we kept asking each other. We felt alive and invincible. It was a miracle that we hadn't killed ourselves that day.

That wouldn't be the last time God spared me from the consequences of a bad decision. Other times, He walked with me through them. When I was seventeen, I had no idea what that meant. I could see now, some forty years later, that even when I was hell-bent on doing whatever I wanted, God was present.

I pulled up outside the condo and parked almost in front of the door on the nearly empty street. I grabbed my bag and walked up the short steps to the porch, gritting my teeth against the bitter cold. Memories of opening doors to condos in Ocean City flashed through my mind. I'd done it for countless beach getaways with Tina, and later Marcus and Christina in tow.

I was alone now. I pushed the thought aside and opened the door. I had escaped to the solitude I'd been longing for, but now I wondered if getting away from it all was what I needed. *Would I hear from God here?*

I stepped inside and visions kept coming of happier times spent down the shore with Tina, and Marcus, and Christina. How sweet those days of building our family and enjoying each other's company had been. Tina loved Christmas. Now, I would be here, alone through Christmas and New Year's. No tree, no lights. With Tina and Christina gone, Marcus and I hadn't even gotten our tree out after Thanksgiving the way we'd always done. I felt trapped by my grief and loss, and the need for escape had driven me to this familiar place in the dead of winter. I let my thoughts drift back over poor choices I had made in the past when I'd felt trapped, desperate to escape my circumstances.

A year or two after I graduated from high school, the consequences of bad decisions I was making with drugs and women were piling up. I had seen the recruiting ads on tv promising that the Navy was not just a job, but an adventure.

Ocean City, Marcus and Christina building castles in the sand

I decided to get away from it all by enlisting. I walked into the recruiting office in Berlin, not far from where we lived and sat down with the recruiting officer, "Hoppy" Hopkins.

Hoppy went over the program with me and answered all my questions. He nudged me to take the entry exam and promised he could show me my score that same afternoon. So, I took the written test right then and there. After I'd finished, Hoppy scored the test and told me that I'd passed. He said he'd have the results of the aptitude tests in the morning.

That next day Hoppy called to say I'd done well on the aptitude test and that I had many options as far as where I could serve. He invited me to come back to the office so he could explain, and when I arrived he was excited to tell me that I'd scored high enough to be accepted into the Navy's nuclear program. I could go to school for four to six months before being assigned to a ship. The anti-nuclear energy movement was gaining momentum in the 70s, and I had seen news coverage of sit-ins protesting its use. Demonstrators tried to convince the public how dangerous it was, so because of the growing stigma, I was not thrilled about working with nuclear equipment. Hoppy also told me that I'd have to enlist for six years instead of the usual four if I joined the nuclear program.

I was much more comfortable with the other option he presented, which was to enlist in the area of Electronics and Communication. I would go to Basic Electronics and then Interior Communications school, both of which were in San Diego, California. That got my attention. Ever since graduating high school, I'd felt trapped by my life. I had been in "getaway mode." I even listened to "*Getaway*" by Earth, Wind, & Fire all the time and called it my theme song. Traveling to California sounded like an intriguing way out to me, so in April I signed up for a delayed entry program that would land me in boot camp in San Diego the following October.

Bud and Marcus, happier times

Bud, Edgewood HS Eagles basketball

When I told my parents I was joining the Navy, my mom was sad that I was leaving, but she liked the Navy and always supported me. She was the kind of mom who would sit at the kitchen table with my friends from high school and just talk to them and listen to them. My dad had been in the Army, and he was all for me enlisting in the military. He said the Navy would be good for me. For the next six months, I had a story to tell and an adventure to look forward to. I felt as though the sky was the limit.

Chapter Six

Getaway to the Navy

In the six months leading up to the day I left for boot camp I made loads of bad decisions.

When the time came for me to leave, my dad drove me to the recruiting office in Berlin before dawn. I was beginning to realize how much I was going to miss my parents. My dad and I hugged for a long time outside the recruiting office.

At that time, MEPS–the Military Entrance Processing Station–was located in Philadelphia. Hoppy drove me there, where I'd take the oath of enlistment with about a hundred other recruits. Before the ceremony I met Tom McClennen, the only other guy who was headed to San Diego Naval Base. After the day's activities, he and I eventually boarded a red-eye headed west. It was the first time I'd ever flown on a plane.

We landed at San Diego International Airport at around midnight, where we were instructed to wait for the military transport that would pick us up and take us to the barracks. We sat on the curb outside the airport for hours until the van arrived, then we were hustled inside and off to San Diego Naval Base, a hub for submarine and communications commands.

On base we were driven to a huge, dark hangar and ushered inside. Once my eyes adjusted, I could make out rows and rows of bunks filled with sleeping recruits.

Left: Bud joined the U.S. Navy in 1978

I found my bunk, stashed the few belongings I'd been allowed to bring with me under it, and dropped like a stone onto the narrow berth. It felt like as soon as my head hit the pillow, the boot camp instructor blew open the metal doors and stormed into the barracks kicking what sounded like about forty metal trash cans up and down the aisles. The noise sent recruits, including me, flying up from the bunks to stand, shocked and disoriented before being herded into groups and marched out to get our hair buzzed off.

Afterward, we were paraded past jeering recruits who'd already been through the routine. They were only too happy to make fun of us on our way to the awful breakfast that awaited.

No more than a day or two of this and I knew I'd cavalierly made the biggest mistake of my young life. The Navy, the military, was not for me. I told the recruit in charge of the rest of us that I wanted to speak to the Chaplain. The look on his face made it clear that he thought I was a loser. He sent me to the Chaplain's office.

"I can't do this," I said. *"I made a mistake. I want out."*

"It's too late for that," the Chaplain said. *"Unless you want a dishonorable discharge. That's your choice."*

I sat in the chair across from the Chaplain and felt the weight of my careless decision slowly bear down on me, squeezing the breath from my lungs. My dad's words rang in my ears. Once again, I was free to choose and bear the consequences.

"You can make a phone call," the Chaplain said.

I grabbed that lifeline. I called my dad, fully expecting him to rescue me.

"Dad, this ain't for me," I bellyached. *"I made a mistake. I just want to get out."*

My dad answered with the same steady, matter-of-fact voice that had spoken the words that freed me to decide whether or not I would continue to go to church and set me on the journey to make my own choices.

"Stop your crying, and be a man," he said.

And with that, he hung up.

***

I put my bag on the floor in the living room and headed for the kitchen. The condo was a good size, but being here alone, it felt huge. There was too much space for just me. Tina had a larger-than-life presence, and her absence left a gaping hole. The thought that I could do whatever I wanted now wasn't comforting. It was scary.

Lord, I've walked with you all these years, and I don't want to stop now. But I could. I could just start drifting away, or drinking, or pornography or hanging with whomever, doing whatever–just numb myself.

There in the condo I prayed and really reached out to God. I thought back to the first time I heard the gospel and believed it.

In the summer of '77 I got a job at Overbrook Senior High School helping to clean, paint, and get the place ready for the next school year. I remember going to work the first day and finding out that a guy named Tom Horner also worked there. I almost quit on the spot.

Tom was best friends with my cousin Paul, whose younger brother Gary and I were born just nine days apart. Gary and I were as close as two peas in a pod and always called each other, "Cuz." We did just about everything together, and we were always following after Paul. He was like a teenage idol to us. He was always better at basketball, and he was smarter and cooler. Gary and I were the little brothers who hung around in his shadow. We just wanted to be with him, to be like him.

While Cuz and I were still in high school, Paul, Tom, and another guy named Dave had gone to this place called Ranch. It was actually a church where they spent a lot of time singing and talking about Jesus. Cuz and I joked that they'd turned into holy rollers. We couldn't believe it when the three of them graduated and decided to go to Florida Bible College.

When they came home their first summer from college, the transformation was complete. They'd turned into full-fledged Bible thumpers. They walked around with Bibles under their arms, handing out tracts and asking perfect strangers, *"Do you know where you're going when you die?"*

Cuz couldn't escape his brother, but as much as it hurt not to hang out with him and follow Paul around, I did everything I could to avoid the holy rollers. I just didn't want to be with them.

So, when I walked into my summer job at Overbrook Senior High and saw Tom Horner was working there, it was all I could do to stand there and not run screaming from the building. Then the boss tells me Tom and I will be partners, working together, day in and day out. I dreaded going to work. I knew it was coming, that sooner or later Tom was going to start in on me with the Bible thumping. He had just come back from Florida Bible College, and he was on a mission.

And sure enough, one day, right in the middle of work Tom hands me this Bible tract. It was called, *"Are You Going to Heaven?"* I had never seen one before. It even came with a little pencil.

"I ain't got time to look at this, right now, Tom," I said, trying to give the tract and little pencil back to him.

"Okay, whenever you get a chance," he said.

"I'll look at it when I get home," I said, and shoved everything in my pocket.

Later that night, after dinner, I was emptying my pockets in my room when I saw the tract again. I was ready to throw it away, but then I thought, "*You know what, let me just look at it, so I can tell him I did.*"

The tract itself was a tri-fold piece of paper, kind of small. I opened it up and a little checklist caught my eye. It was a list of activities like attending church, following the Ten Commandments, doing good deeds, etc. with little boxes next to them where I could check off which things I thought would get me into Heaven. So I started checking off boxes, feeling confident that I was pretty good, definitely on my way.

Then I turned the page, and the second panel of the tract systematically dismantled all of the assumptions I'd made. Every activity I'd checked off was paired with a Bible verse that explained how there was nothing I could do to earn a place in Heaven. I was mortified.

I kept reading, frantically searching the tract for something the Bible said would save me from burning in Hell. Then I read Ephesians 2:8 and 9, *"By grace you are saved through faith, and that not of yourselves, it is a gift from God,"* and

John 3:16, *"For God so loved the world that He gave His only begotten Son, that whoever believes in him will not perish, but have everlasting life."* I couldn't believe those two were in the Bible. *That can't be right,* I thought. *How does anyone receive a gift just by believing they do? That's just a made up thing.*

I knew my mom had this big Bible in her room, sitting on a little table at the foot of the bed. It was almost like a showpiece. I went in and got that Bible and took it back to my room. I sat on my bed and just fumbled through the pages until I found John 3:16. I had a reverence for God and the Bible–or so I thought–but I had never really looked at one. I couldn't believe that I could go to Heaven just by believing. *This can't be.* I shook my head in disbelief and started looking for the other one.

I was sure there couldn't be anything about faith being a gift from God in the Bible. I had never heard the word before, but I found Ephesians, and I found chapter two, verses 8 and 9. And there it was, an idea that had never occurred to me: *we are saved by grace through faith. And that faith is not our own, but it is a gift from God, not the result of anything we do...so no one can boast about doing anything to earn it.* I could hardly believe that those words had been in the Bible the whole time–that getting to Heaven, being saved from Hell is by God's grace through faith, and this faith is a gift. I was stunned. What shook me most was not only that God would save me, but that I no longer had to hide from Him. I saw for myself that it was written in the Bible. For the first time in my life, I saw that the problem was not that I needed to try harder. I needed God.

I started asking my friends, *"Do you know that the Bible teaches that it's just about what we believe? We don't have to be perfect, because we can't–"*

That was about all I knew, but I was sharing it with everybody. *"Do you know where you're going when you die?"* All of a sudden I realized my friends at school were starting to look at me the way I used to look at Tom.

"You're going off the deep end on us. Why are you talking about death all the time? Why even talk about this anymore?"

My excitement about knowing I was going to Heaven only reminded them of death and dying. No one wanted to think we were anything short of invincible; teenagers taking risks like doing illegal drugs and flying down the highway of life at a hundred miles an hour, much the same way Burley and I had raced along

Route 73 in his Duster and my Corvair. My high school friends seemed to think they could beat death like I'd avoided that slow-moving truck on the highway. So I backed off and went low-key about my newfound faith.

I could always talk to Cuz about spiritual things, though. Neither of us knew much, but I think he was more receptive because he was hearing a lot about God from his brother, Paul. When Tom Horner started hosting men's Bible study on Tuesday nights in the basement of Garden Lake Church, Paul mentioned it to us. I was still smoking pot beforehand with the guys I hooped with, so sometimes I'd be a little buzzed, but I went a couple times anyway, since I told Cuz I would.

Tom was also sharing the gospel with kids our age. Because he worked at the school, he was able to open the gym for basketball games on Saturday nights from 7 pm to 9 pm. Everyone was welcome, but Tom had one requirement. We'd play ball for an hour, then at 8:00 we'd break for drinks and snacks. Tom and Paul were now both married, and their wives Sharon and Linda made cookies and lemonade. During that break, everyone had to listen to Tom share the gospel, which I learned meant, *"Good news."*

I started going, mostly to play basketball. The games were competitive, and there were always at least ten or so guys there. We'd play, then Tom would give the gospel message in a brief, impactful way that was easy to remember. One of my favorites was when he'd hold up his hands, empty palms facing the group as we sat on the bleachers enjoying the snacks.

"Let's say this hand represents you and me, the whole world," he'd say, pushing his left hand forward. He'd reach around and take his wallet from his back pocket and put it in his left hand.

"This wallet represents our sin," he'd say. *"We all have sin. The whole world is affected by sin."*

Then, raising his right hand, he'd say, *"Let this hand represent Jesus Christ. The Bible teaches that God so loved the world that He gave His one and only Son Jesus, that whoever would believe in him would never perish, but have everlasting life."*

And then he'd take the wallet with his right hand.

"So Jesus took the sin of the whole world. He died and was buried, and rose again," he'd say, putting the wallet in his back pocket and holding up his empty right hand, *"offering eternal life for those who believe."*

That was the simple message Tom shared. That message was getting drilled into me every Saturday night, even while I dreamed of escaping the trappings of my small town New Jersey life.

By joining the Navy, I had lived up to my theme song, *"Getaway"* and escaped everything–my family, my small home town, boring church services, all of it. But instead of feeling euphoric, I was at the end of myself. I'd heard people at church say that when they just didn't know what to do. I imagined this is what it felt like. I was between a rock and a hard place with two choices: I could either stick it out for eight weeks of boot camp and what I was sure would be four long, scary years of Navy life, or be sent home with a dishonorable discharge. I couldn't bear the thought of disappointing my parents. Somehow, I found the strength to put my nose to the grindstone and get through it. I poured myself into training and studying, and pushed forward.

My forced commitment had unexpected benefits. There were two guys in our unit who always scored highest on the grueling academic tests we took regularly as part of basic training. My scores always ranked third, but no more than a couple of points behind the two of them, so when it was time to take the final exam, they were sure they were only competing with each other for the top spot. After the exam, our instructor announced the test scores and to their surprise, and mine, not only had I outscored the two of them, I had aced the final and earned the Academic Award for our class.

Looking back, I realize that my circumstance and my desperation had forced me to grow. I drew on a strength that I didn't know was available to me. I was a scared, depressed kid who was certain I'd made the worst mistake of my life. I would have done just about anything to escape the hell I'd gotten myself into. I didn't know it while I was struggling through boot camp, but those few Tuesday nights at men's Bible study in the basement of Tom's church and Saturday nights between basketball games before I'd enlisted had taken root somewhere within me. Even then I was learning—failure did not have the final word.

Bud Sr., Caroline, Bud Jr. (holding nephew Nicky) and Carole on deck of USS Guadalcanal

I know now that God was helping me, though it would be years before I knew enough to realize that it was Him. In countless situations after that, God would show me that the strength to keep going–the strength that seems to come out of nowhere–is Him walking with me and, sometimes, carrying me.

After basic training I went home for two weeks, then it was back to San Diego for Basic Electricity Electronics class. Basic training classes had been grueling, but BEE nearly broke me. I remember taking the final exam and immediately heading to the men's bathroom afterward. I felt like crying my heart out, certain I'd bombed the test. If I failed now, my Navy career would consist of polishing brass or swabbing the decks.

Thankfully, I passed the exam, pretty much by the skin of my teeth. I was cleared for A School, which I passed with flying colors. I was excited to be doing something in the world, accomplishing goals–even though I'd begun my time in the Navy on a whim and had gotten off on a shaky start.

After I graduated from A School, I was assigned to the USS Guadalcanal. I proudly received my orders, printed on green and white barred computer paper complete with spool holes down the sides for feeding it through the printer. I was excited to be a sailor and looking forward to my first tour of duty.

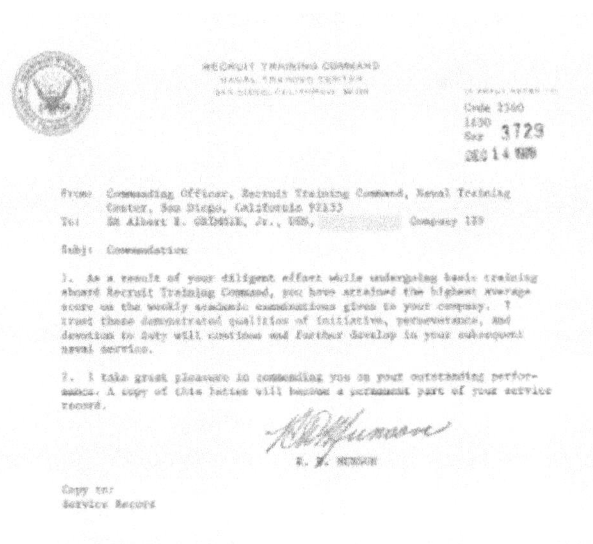

RECRUIT TRAINING COMMAND
[illegible]

Code 3300
1650
Ser 3729
[illegible]

From: Commanding Officer, Recruit Training Command, Naval Training Center, San Diego, California 92133
To: SR Albert [illegible], Jr., USN, Company 139

Subj: Commendation

1. As a result of your diligent effort while undergoing basic training aboard Recruit Training Command, you have attained the highest average score on the weekly academic examinations given to your company. I trust these demonstrated qualities of initiative, perseverance, and devotion to duty will continue and further develop in your subsequent naval service.

2. I take great pleasure in commending you on your outstanding performance. A copy of this letter will become a permanent part of your service record.

[illegible]

Copy to:
Service Record

Bud's Academic Award letter

But first, I was allowed to go home for a couple of weeks on leave. It was great to be home celebrating with family and friends. I had stories to tell, achievements under my belt, and a new outlook on life.

About a week in I started to fall in with the old familiar crowd. I smoked some and reconnected with an old flame or two. I always felt guilty afterward, like I'd let God down. I didn't want to do that, and I didn't want to fall too far back into habits I knew would lead to no good. I liked my new life as a sailor. I was proud of the things I'd accomplished, and I wanted to keep that feeling. I wanted to permanently leave my old vices behind, but it didn't seem like I had the will or strength to resist temptation for very long. I started to realize that I didn't need a few habits cleaned up. I needed a different heart.

Onboard ship, any time I mentioned belief in the Bible, or my faith in God, even generally, the push back made me feel like I was in high school all over again. Nobody wanted to hear any of it. I started to wonder if the Bible stories and my faith were just a fairytale, after all.

I bought a copy of a book called *Contradictions of the Bible*. I was a skeptic, determined to prove the Bible was just a bunch of made up stories that shouldn't rule my life. I didn't need God looking over my shoulder like some sort of "sky dad." My parents had done their job. They watched over me, and cared for me, and took me to church. But that afternoon, when he said I didn't have to go to church any more if I didn't want to, Dad freed me to make my own choices about life, about church and about what kind of relationship I would have with God–or whether I would have one at all.

Although I picked up *Contradictions of the Bible* with the goal of discrediting the Bible, the more I read, the more I noticed holes in the authors' arguments. I began to see the validity of the Scriptures, but I needed to make sure the Bible actually said what the authors claimed it did. I didn't run out and buy a Bible of my own, though.

There was so much to learn about my job in Internal Communications now that I was aboard ship, I didn't have the energy or the inclination to put in the effort to debunk the book. I was already studying non-stop for exams and apprenticing under other seamen to learn how to do my job in the IC department.

On top of that, Jack and Basil, a couple of guys who outranked me, took every opportunity to ride me as a newbie, especially if I brought up anything about God, or church, or my faith. I decided it wasn't worth it trying to talk about God with them around. Once again, the same as I had back in boot camp, I put my nose to the grindstone and just did my job. I focused on succeeding in the Navy. I didn't want to be a slug. I was determined to become the best sailor I could be.

Eventually, I earned the rank of Petty Officer, 3rd Class. Around that time a guy named Tom LaTina came on board. He and I were the same rank, so we shared similar duties and worked together often. Over time we got to know each other, and at some point I mentioned that I was going to the chapel for services on Sunday. Tom said he planned to go as well, and from then on we started casually talking about God and faith. I opened up about the *Contradictions* book and about not really trusting a lot of what I'd been reading. I told Tom that I didn't have a Bible, so I'd just sort of given up figuring things out for the moment. Tom didn't have any answers, either, but it was nice to have someone to at least talk about spiritual things with who wasn't just trying to attack the idea of religion or God.

Tom and I worked together for a couple months before he went home on leave for two weeks. When he came back aboard the U.S.S. Guadalcanal, he was a new man. While he was home he'd gone to church, heard the gospel message, and accepted Jesus as his Lord and Savior. He was completely transformed. Jack and Basil started calling him, "*Eyewitness Tom.*" Pretty soon it caught on with the whole crew.

"Slim," —my shipmates nicknamed me that because I was tall and lanky. *"I understand, now,"* Tom said, brandishing a thick, brown leather book that had "Holy Bible" stamped on its cover. The pages were gold-leafed like the ones in the big Bible at the foot of my mother's bed.

Tom's voice broke into my distraction. *"Jesus died on the cross for our sins!"* he said. *"If we believe in him, He takes away everything that would stop us from going to Heaven when we die!"*

His face was beaming. He clapped me on the shoulder.

"This is for you," he said, shoving the Bible into my hands. *"I got one just like it. We can read, and pray, and spread the gospel all over the ship."*

"Wow, thanks, Tom," I said. I appreciated the gesture. He'd bought me my very first Bible. I was excited to finally be able to read the Scriptures for myself.

But I also felt like I was back in high school, tempted to run away from "holy roller" Tom Horner, grinning and asking if I knew where I was going after I died.

Bud on leave after boot camp

Chapter Seven

Seeking God on the Guadalcanal

I hadn't bothered to turn the lights on in the condo. As I sat there in the dim light of the kitchen, I had the same disconcerting feeling I had right after Tina's death–that I could easily blow my life up. Tina had been my guardrail. Without her, I was tempted to venture off the familiar road of faith we'd traveled together. I had no idea where my journey with God was headed. I'd seen many men get sidetracked and slowly drift away from God and their families after experiencing far less hurt and pain than I had. I thought of my son, Marcus, and I couldn't bear the thought of letting him down.

Suddenly, I remembered the 100-day goal journal Tony had given me as an early Christmas gift. I walked to the living room and dug the book out of my bag. I held it in my hands and read, *"Accomplish what matters."*

I turned the lights on and sat down on the couch. Traveling back through my memories and looking to God for guidance was turning into an ongoing discussion in my mind between Him and me. The words of Proverbs 3:5 floated up in my thoughts.

Trust in the Lord with all your heart ...

After John 3:16 and Ephesians 2:8-9, it was one of the first Bible verses I memorized. I'd worked on it while walking Tina's German shepherd, Tippy, outside our first apartment in Voorhees.

Okay, I'll just jump into this. God, what does *matter most to me right now?*

That was the right question.

It's probably a good time to start that workout thing and stay healthy. I'm tempted to just let myself go.

But that's not the most important thing. That's not what matters most.

I could get going on the book I've been wanting to write. In one hundred days I could get a really good start on it.

But again, Lord, that's not what I want most.

I know–I want to organize my life–my finances, my filing cabinets...just put everything in good order.

That ain't it, either.

Then it came to me. I jotted the thought down in the 100-day goal journal so I wouldn't forget.

"I want to be the best man I can possibly be for you, God. Because you'll help me with this pain that I have."

The USS Guadalcanal

The Bible Tom LaTina had given me back aboard the Guadalcanal was a King James version, and I struggled to understand the English. I later picked up another book called *Evidence That Demands a Verdict* by Josh McDowell to help sort things out. Back then, I wanted to learn and understand all I could about what had so resonated with me from the little tract Tom Horner gave that summer after high school–I needed God, and He accepted me. I was going to Heaven because of His grace and what He did for me.

All these years later, alone in Ocean City, I thought about my relationship with God. After losing first Christina, and now Tina, I felt like my best friend had kicked me in the teeth–twice. Tina and I had weathered her cancer and Christina's death together. Now I was alone. What kind of relationship could I have with God after He had allowed me to suffer so much pain and loss?

I wasn't sure exactly what this next phase of my journey with God would look like, but I showered and got ready for bed that night confident that He was with me. I felt the tiny spark of something I hadn't felt since Tina died. I felt hope–for myself. I was not going to blow up my life.

I've always been drawn to sunrises. The next morning in the condo, I awoke to sunshine streaming through the blinds of the bedroom window. It felt like a harbinger of better things to come. A new day had dawned, and I was exactly where I needed to be. I stretched out my arms and exhaled long and slow, overwhelmed by a feeling of peace and marveling at God's perfect timing. Suddenly, my memories didn't feel like dark waves threatening to pull me down into the depths of despair. Instead, I was eager to be refreshed and renewed by whatever God would say to me through them.

Over the next two weeks, the running dialogue between God and me would help rebuild my faith and trust. It would begin to renew my relationship with Him and give me the strength to push forward.

I started the 100-day goal journal, and over time it became too small to hold all the thoughts, and prayers, and notes, and all the things I talked to God about. I bought yet another notebook and began recording just about everything that happened in my life and my thoughts about the truths God had revealed to me over the course of my life.

I also decided to read the whole Bible, from Genesis to Revelation. I had been a believer for more than thirty years, but had only half-heartedly done it with Cuz when I was younger. I skimmed through some parts, like the Book of Leviticus, which read to me like a long, boring list of do's and don'ts, but this time would be different. I came across some videos from the Bible Project that were really helpful. There were short summaries of each book, and videos that pointed out and explained recurring themes throughout the Bible. And this time I didn't just read; I listened and followed along to the familiar voice of Max McLean reading the Scripture aloud. I would begin each morning in Ocean City eager to pray and listen for God in my developing routine.

Bud, Guadalcanal Uniform Site TV

All those years ago when I was in the Navy, I had begun to really seek God for myself. I would talk about God and the Bible with Tom LaTina and Miles Hamilton, also a believer who served with us aboard the Guadalcanal, and later Rick "Gib" Gibson, another crewman. Rick and I were similar in temperament and became good friends; I was part of his wedding party. "Eyewitness Tom" came off like James and John, Jesus' disciples known in the New Testament as the Sons of Thunder because of their zeal for Christ, but Miles was more diplomatic in his approach. He would take advantage of conversations or situations that seemed to naturally lend themselves to talking about spiritual things.

Bud in the IC department

I admired the way Miles shared the gospel so effortlessly, but for the most part I still kept my faith under wraps aboard ship. I felt like I always had one foot on a path toward God, but the other foot was still inclined in the direction of getting high, swearing like a proverbial sailor, and–just like I had in high school–doing just about whatever it took to try to fit in.

Naturally, a ship full of men frequently held conversations about women. Guys were always bragging about their conquests and prowess–real or imagined. I had a friend back home named Wendy who would always write me encouraging letters about Jesus and growing in the faith. As soon as my shipmates saw that I was getting mail they let fly with the usual comments and innuendos.

"Hey Slim, you got a girlfriend?"

Instead of telling the truth, I let the crew think what they wanted–pretty much that Wendy was my girlfriend. I also didn't correct their estimations of how many girls I'd fooled around with. I was no altar boy, but I was willing to let their speculations run rampant just to feel like one of the guys.

I spent five years in the Navy and was honorably discharged on May 4, 1984. Back home, I was still smoking cigarettes and pot, but on Tuesday nights I was also going to Tom Horner's Bible study in the basement of Garden Lake Church. Each week Tom would have one of the students lead a short devotional to kick things off before Bible study, and he would incorporate that devotional message into the lesson. Everyone knew that when Tom reached under his chair and pulled out his calendar he was getting ready to "volunteer" someone to lead a devotional the following week. I remember the first time Tom called on me to do it.

"Okay, who wants to do devotion?"

Tom reached under his chair, and I busied myself with the toe of my shoe. Out of the corner of my eye, I saw him opening the calendar. I intently studied a random pattern I'd discovered in the tile on the floor, all the while thinking, "Don't look at me, Tom."

"Okay, Bud," Tom said. "I'll put you down for next Tuesday."

Preparing to lead that five or ten minute devotional was the beginning of my Bible study life in earnest. I bought my first notebook, what's now the old-fashioned three-ring binder kind with a cloth cover. In the top right corner I wrote "Psalm 143:8."

"Let me hear your loving devotion in the morning, for I have put my trust in You. Teach me the way I should walk, for to You I lift up my soul."

I spent the whole week researching and actually reading and studying the Scriptures. At the end of it, I was totally over-prepared to talk for just five minutes, but I had gotten so much out of it.

I'd first really talked to 'Cuz, Paul, and Tom Horner about salvation in my teens. Then, I talked more about faith with Tom, Miles, and Gib. During that time I began to realize my deep need for fellowship with men, though ultimately, Tina had been the person I talked to about the deepest spiritual things.

I had trusted God through thirty-one years of marriage, and I had learned so much through many trials, tears, and triumphs–but always with Tina in my mind and heart. Now, I was a widower. A single man. Sitting in a rented condo in Ocean City, surrounded by memories of years that seemed to have gone by too fast, it was just me and God. He was the One I needed to talk to the most. I'd come here to be alone in His presence, and He had been speaking to me every day about His love and devotion.

I no longer felt hopeless, but I still felt lost. I existed in a kind of limbo, suspended between the life I'd had in the past with my family and this place of not knowing what to do next, or what my life was supposed to look like.

"Lord, if it's just You and me for the rest of my days, I am content with that."

I sat bolt upright on the couch in the living room. I had surrendered to God with these words before, and His response changed my life forever.

Chapter Eight

Head Meets Heart

The year was 1987. I was 28 years old and going through the motions in another crash-and-burn relationship. Four years out of the Navy, I wondered if I was destined to be single all my life. I was decidedly a Christian by that time, and I had been attending men's Bible study with Tom Horner, Cuz, and Paul at Garden Lake Church most Tuesday nights for the past few years. The things of God occupied a prominent place in my life, including wanting to find the right person, get married, and raise a family. With that in mind, I eventually called it quits on my latest relationship that was going nowhere.

One night, I sat cross-legged on my bed with my Bible open. I started thinking about the years that had passed since I first understood God's gift of salvation through faith. Lamenting the way my romantic life seemed to be unfolding, I slipped into heartfelt prayer to God. I remember feeling strongly that if I really trusted Him, I could be confident that He would never leave me alone. In fact, His word convinced me–He loved me enough to come into the world and die in my place, so that I could be with Him forever.

I remember the moment vividly. I was okay with being done with dating for a while. For once, I was no longer trying to arrange my own future. I was handing it over to God. I said the words to Him out loud.

"Lord, if it's just You and me for the rest of my days, I'm content with that."

Left: Bud and Tina, a sailor and his girl

I had been working at TriStar Data Systems in Cherry Hill for the past three years, but the next morning I went to work feeling like a new day had dawned in my life. I felt peace and contentment about my future in a way I never had before.

I walked into the break room, where a co-worker, Tom Antonelli, sat drinking coffee before our shift. I'd interviewed and recommended the company hire Tom, and we'd become friends since he started working at TriStar.

"Hey, Bud, do you have a girlfriend?" Tom asked.

I had lied about having a girlfriend back in the Navy. And I'd been in too many relationships that had gone too far, too fast, only to end up nowhere. On the heels of my heart-to-heart with God the night before, I was ready to give dating a break for a while. Maybe indefinitely.

"No, I don't have a girlfriend," I said. *"As a matter of fact, I have just come to terms with being single."*

It felt good to give a completely honest answer about the state of my lovelife.

"And I am happy to say there are no skeletons in my closet," I said as I walked to the counter and poured myself a cup of coffee. *"No lingering female relationships to complicate things."*

I felt like a clean slate, fresh and new, comfortable in my unmarried, unattached state.

"Would you want to meet someone?" Tom asked. *"I know a girl named Tina. The other day she said something you always say. It got me thinking–I should introduce you to each other."*

I don't think I hesitated or even gave the idea a second thought.

"Yes," I said. *"Sure, why not?*

***

Little did I know, Tina hadn't been as eager about being set up on a blind date.

"I don't want to meet any guy right now, Tom!" Tina said. *"Forget it!"*

"This guy goes to church," Tom said.

"So what? A lot of guys go to church." Tina wasn't impressed.

"He reads his Bible," Tom said.

"Really?" That got her attention. *"How do you know?"*

It was just like Tina to demand evidence. She didn't just take people's word for anything.

"Well, he talks about it a lot," Tom said. *"And, like you, he talked about it even when I didn't know him that well."*

I smiled, relaxing back into the couch. All these years later, I was so thankful that Tom hadn't given up, and that Tina had eventually agreed to the date–but not before insisting she'd bring her wingman along.

"I'll go, but I'm bringing Laura with me!"

Tom invited Tina and me to meet at one of his street hockey games over in National Park, about 25 minutes from where I lived with my parents. I decided to bring my ten-year-old nephew, Nicky, along. We got to the rink just as the game was starting and slid in next to a few other people leaning on the boards to see the action up close. I was looking around for possible Tina sightings, but I realized that since I'd never met her, I wouldn't recognize her, anyway.

A few minutes later I noticed two girls getting out of a car and walking toward the street hockey rink. They had walked straight up to the boards and leaned in about 10 or so feet to the right of Nicky and me, when the ball came flying out of the rink between us. One of the two girls took off like a shot after it. She chased the ball down and threw it back to one of the refs in the rink for a faceoff to restart play. I was mesmerized.

"Thanks, Tina!" Tom yelled from behind his mask.

I couldn't talk to her fast enough.

"So, you must be Tina," I said, and introduced myself.

After the game, Tom suggested we all get lunch at Pizza Pronto on the White Horse Pike in Somerdale.

We grabbed a table and made small talk while we waited to order.

"Do you play street hockey?" Tina asked.

"No, I actually play basketball," I said. *"If you like, you could come to one of my games this week."*

I didn't know it at the time, but Tina had vowed never to date jocks. She'd had bad experiences with too many. She was kicking Laura under the table while I tried to impress her with the fact that I played in three different basketball leagues.

"Well, what else do you do?" Laura asked.

"I work for a computer company," I said. *"And I was in the Navy for five years before that."*

"Have you actually been to sea?" Tina asked. I thought I noticed her leaning in slightly.

"Yes," I said. *"I served aboard ship for four of those years."*

Tina started to nudge Laura with her elbow, but ended up knocking over her purse. It hit the tile with a clatter and stuff spilled out. Quick as a wink, Tina was under the table scooping up the contents of her purse, all the while keeping the conversation going. Suddenly, her head popped up from under the table, her face flushed and hair disheveled. She smoothed it down and flashed a smile in my direction.

I found out later that Tina had always wanted to fall in love and marry a Navy man, like her dad.

Sitting in the living room of the condo in Ocean City, I laughed the way Tina and I had every time we shared the story of how we met.

***

The next day I drove to Pizza Pronto for lunch.

The parking lot looked uncharacteristically empty, but I had pulled all the way in and was making my way to the door when I realized the place was closed—not for the afternoon, but permanently, as in gone out of business.

I stood still, resisting the temptation to reach out my hand and try the door. It felt like the wind had been knocked out of me. Tina and I had practically met here. For Pizza Pronto to be closed seemed like a huge chunk of my life, of what made me, *me* had been swallowed up in a black hole.

I walked back to the car and sat, stunned, alternately staring into the windows of the empty building or off into space, seeing nothing. Thoughts of those first days with Tina filled my mind, surrounded me in the car. We seemed destined to be together from the start. After that day at Pizza Pronto we were almost inseparable. We'd both been through enough bad relationships to recognize we had something special, and neither of us wanted to let it go.

I missed her terribly. From the moment I saw her, Tina lit up my whole world.

A tear popped into the corner of my eye, and I brushed it away. She lit up everything she touched. I smiled. Sometimes like a fireball.

Tina came into the world with the spark of her Romanian father and fire of her Italian mother in her spirit. And she kept it. Tina was passionate, fiercely loyal, deeply compassionate, and unfiltered in the most honest way.

Anyone who knew Tina knew exactly where they stood. That day at the street hockey game I'd fumbled introducing myself after Tom called out to Tina, thanking her for throwing the bright orange ball back into play.

"I'm Bud," I said. *"You must be Tina."*

After we'd been dating for a couple months, Tina told me what she'd really been thinking at the time.

"No shit, Sherlock. You must be brilliant!"

I know some people couldn't get past her strong personality. But anyone who truly got to know Tina couldn't help but love her. She was so much like her Grandmom Milos—an iron fist in a velvet glove with a heart of gold.

I pictured Grandmom Milos' dark eyes, set in a face that was still smooth, even though she had to be in her eighties when I met her. She was a steady presence in Tina's life. A survivor who came from humble beginnings in her homeland and often worked more than one job at a time after immigrating to the United States, she was tough. But for Tina, Grandmom Milos was love embodied. She taught Tina what care looked like, what gentleness felt like, and how much it meant to make someone feel safe and special. Even in the midst of her parents' betrayal, Tina clung to her grandmother's example. She chased love because through her Grandmom Milos, she had seen it first hand.

When her parents refused to allow her to return home after ending her marriage to Billy, Tina spent several nights in her car with her faithful German shepherd, Tippy by her side. Eventually she swallowed her pride and reached out to Grandmom Milos. Her grandmother welcomed Tina into her home in Philadelphia with open arms.

Shortly after, her older cousin Bobby joined them, and for the first time in years, Tina felt like she had a real family. Grandmom Milos' home became her refuge, and Bobby became a spiritual mentor to her.

Young Grandmom Milos, circa 1900

Tina always looked up to Bobby. She adored him. He encouraged her to let go of the objects she'd clung to for comfort—dream books, horoscopes, statues—and she listened. He told her to get rid of those things and instead turn to the Bible. She began reading the Psalms and felt a glimmer of peace she hadn't known since she'd heard about God's love at vacation bible school. Bobby reminded her of the simple truth she'd learned as a little girl: God's love and salvation weren't earned–they were a gift from Him, freely given.

Tina was heartbroken when Bobby died suddenly from a brain injury. Her family history was replete with dysfunction, and Bobby's untimely death deepened her sorrows. Her father, Skip, died of prostate cancer, and her mother, Gina, died of leukemia. One of her uncles committed suicide, another died young, and her Aunt Flo died alone in a nursing home. Tina and I were the only people at her funeral besides the chaplain and cemetery staff. There was no one to mourn her; her husband Larry had died young. They had no children; she had no friends.

In her sorrow, Tina soaked in the Psalms. She clung to their honesty, their raw emotion and unwavering declarations of God's faithfulness. The Psalms gave voice to things she felt but didn't always know how to say. Through David's words she found comfort, courage, and assurance that she wasn't alone in her struggles. Tina loved love. She chased after it with as much abandon as she had chased down the bright ball the day I met her at Tom Antonelli's street hockey game.

My own faith journey had followed a less emotional path. I found myself drawn to Paul's letters, especially the book of Romans. His clear-eyed explanation of grace through faith fascinated me. But just as Tina had done with the Psalms, I soaked Paul's letters in. I studied his arguments, dissected the structure of his theology, and felt my own understanding of the Gospel sharpen and stretch.

We often joked that Tina was the heart, and I was the head. Truthfully, God used both streams to build something strong between us. Tina taught me to love more deeply, and I helped her see how God's love could make sense even when life didn't. Somehow, through our struggles–maybe even because of them–we knew we were meant for each other.

Chapter Nine

After the Bear

Pizza Pronto was closed, but I wasn't ready to go back to the condo just yet. I started the car and left the parking lot, heading nowhere in particular. Memories of being in this place, driving along these streets comforted me.

After that first meeting, Tom did end up bringing Tina to one of my basketball games at the YMCA in Woodbury. They were friends, so the plan was he'd bring her to the game and then take her home afterward. Tina was adamant.

"Tom, you are taking me home," Tina said. *"No two ways about it."*

"Sure," Tom said.

After the game I went over to say hi and thank them for coming to see me play.

"I guess I'll take Tina home," I said.

"Sounds good," Tom said and left before Tina could object.

The memory of that night lingered, and almost without thinking I let the rental car drive me toward the apartment where I'd dropped Tina off.

The car seemed to find its own way to Jackson Drive, in Voorhees. As I drove, my eyes searched for the sign marking the entrance to the development, *Village Apartments.*

Nearly thirty years had passed, but the place looked almost exactly the same.

Following the black asphalt road as it curved around toward the parking lot to the front of what had once been our little one-bedroom apartment felt the same as it had coming home to Tina thousands of times before.

Left: Bud and Tina, meant for each other

I eased the car into a space and shut off the engine. For a moment, I just sat there. The engine went quiet, but the memories did not. They rose up all at once, as if they had been waiting for me in that parking lot the whole time.

I got out of the rental car and walked toward the little wooden bridge where Tina and I had stood so many times together. It was the same bridge we had crossed with Tippy, taking him on walks as we talked about work, bills, church, and all the ordinary pieces of a young marriage.

But we had also dreamed there.

We had stood on that bridge and imagined a future we had not yet seen. A home of our own. Children. A family. A life unfolding beyond that small one-bedroom apartment.

For a few minutes, I let myself stand there again, not just as the man I was now, but as the young husband I had been then. So much had happened since those days. So much joy. So much loss. So much love. And yet the memories were not distant or faded. They felt vivid, almost alive, as if God had preserved them for that very moment.

Tina always said the first year of our marriage was a bear; my heart yearned for the easy joy of those early years that followed. As I walked back to the car, a broad smile spread across my face. I was surprised by it at first, but I did not resist it. My memories held more than pain. They were precious evidence, reminders of the life God had allowed me to live with Tina, with Marcus, with Christina.

I opened the car door with an unexpected excitement rising in me. I headed for Sicklerville, to the condo where our children were born, where our family had truly begun. I could hardly wait to relive the feelings of being there again.

Tina and I were committed to a long-term relationship and marriage almost from the start, but our whirlwind romance was often a roller coaster ride.

Almost from the moment we started dating, Tina made it absolutely clear that she did not want children. Growing up in a broken, dysfunctional home had left deep emotional scars. She wanted no part of repeating the cycle of anger and chaos she'd witnessed in her parents' relationship.

The little wooden bridge

That afternoon watching street hockey, Tina had noticed me there with my nephew, then ten-year-old Nicky, who she thought was my son.

"I was all geared up to let Tom have it," Tina shared with me later. *"The last thing I wanted was to start dating a guy with a kid. But when we went to lunch at Pizza Pronto and I found out Nicky was your nephew—and you were a Navy man—I decided to take a chance on you."*

As our relationship grew, Tina fought hard to break the cycle of dysfunction she'd grown up in. There were arguments. Yelling. Threats of leaving born of the hurt and distrust from her past. Once we were married, she'd scream at me even as I prayed by the side of our bed, then storm out, taking off in her car just as she'd seen her father do countless times when she was a child. But always, and I do mean always, she'd come around. She'd come home, apologizing in humility. During those years we worked on our relationship, emphasizing how to communicate effectively and with love. We tried to do what the Bible says about not letting the sun go down on your anger—a lot.

We attended Bible studies and prayer meetings regularly, hungry to know God and each other better. But when she was hurting, Tina was fearful of becoming what she saw from her own parents, especially when it came to having children.

She started telling me more about her medical history, the endometriosis and the surgery. She shared the doctors' warnings and her own uncertainty about becoming pregnant, doubts she'd carried alone for so long. In the early 70s when she was a teenager the treatments were relatively new, and her doctors weren't confident about her ability to have children afterward. I remember talking with her parents, Gina and Skip about what Tina had gone through. I was trying to understand it better, trying to be strong for her when she felt so weak and hopeless.

Tina would sometimes say, almost defiantly, that she didn't want children anyway. Not because the desire wasn't real deep down, but because hoping felt dangerous after she'd been disappointed so many times before. It was easier for Tina to declare she didn't want children than to admit she did and might never have them.

"I mean it, Bud," she'd say, only half joking, *"If I ever do get married, I will have an attorney draw up papers guaranteeing my husband can never pressure me into having kids."*

I'd just smile and tell her what I knew in my heart.

"Tina, you'd make a wonderful mother," I'd say. "But I would never demand that you have children with me."

She'd just roll her eyes and wave me off. But I knew. It wasn't a guess or a romantic hunch. I truly believed God allowed me to see something in Tina–in the way she longed for affection, and the way she expressed how much she wished her parents had loved her.

Tina may not have had a good model to follow, but deep inside, she knew exactly what a good parent should be–because she'd seen what less than that looked like. She knew what she had missed.

Try as we might, for the first few years of our marriage it looked like Tina and I might not be able to have children of our own. The endometriosis of her teens seemed to have taken its toll on her womb. She might never be able to bring a baby into the world.

But during that time of waiting, I watched as something in Tina began to change. She spent time around my sister Carole's kids and saw the way they loved her, naturally, freely, without hesitation. She met women like my cousin Paul's wife, Linda at Garden Lake Bible Church where we attended, who were wonderful mothers. She watched the way their children ran to them, leaned into them, and trusted them. Tina saw something else too: she saw that those children loved her, and she loved them right back. Something awakened in her, not pressure from me, not a forced decision, but a growing desire that surprised even her. And as her desire grew, so did her prayers.

Tina came home from work one day with exciting news. Her boss at the mortgage company told her about a new development of condos going up for sale in nearby Sicklerville.

By then, we had been married almost two years, and we had begun praying about the possibility of owning a home someday instead of renting. It did not have to be anything grand. We were young, still finding our way, and a brand new condo seemed like the perfect first step, a place that could belong to us while we kept building our life together. So we decided to purchase our first home.

The first two years in that condo were full of energy, laughter, and new beginnings. We were attending Garden Lake Bible Church, hosting prayer meetings in our living room, and making friends both at church and in the development. We met another Christian couple, John and Linda Clegg, while walking our dogs. They lived in the building adjacent to ours and we became fast friends.

Bud and Tina, 1987

Our life seemed to be opening up in every direction. We had secure jobs, were growing in our faith, growing in our marriage, and beginning to understand the joy of creating a home together.

During that season, one of the missionaries from our church, Brian Thomas, began coming to our condo early one morning each week to pray with us. Tina and I had been praying for her to conceive, and this faithful man joined us in that hope. Week after week, he sat with us and prayed, asking God to bless us with a child.

Looking back, I can still see that little condo as more than just our first home. It was a place of beginnings. A place where friendship deepened, faith became more personal, and hope quietly filled the rooms before we ever knew how much those prayers would mean.

I wrote a note about Hannah's prayer in 1 Samuel on a small piece of paper for Tina. Hannah was a woman in the Bible who was barren, and she poured her grief out to God so deeply that even the priest misunderstood her at first. She wasn't polished or calm. She was honest. She wept and pleaded, promising that if God gave her a child, she would dedicate that child to Him.

Tina kept that little paper. I remember seeing it at different times over the years. I made a mental note to look for it when I got back home to LA. It represented something sacred in my family's story: a quiet marker of how desperate prayer can become a lifeline.

I thought about the many heart-to-heart talks Tina and I had in those days. We wanted children, yes, but we also wanted to trust God's plans for us. In our struggle with infertility, we were learning what it means to trust Him when you can't control the outcome. Tina prayed for long hours, with tears. There were nights when the only thing I could do was sit beside her and hold her hand, because words weren't enough.

And then she got pregnant.

I remember exactly where I was when she called and told me the home test was positive. For a moment it felt like the sky opened and the world finally made sense. We were stunned. So grateful, laughing and crying at the same time.

Her gynecologist, Dr. Pogorski confirmed the pregnancy, but complications came quickly. It was an ectopic pregnancy. The embryo had implanted in the fallopian tube and would have to be removed surgically. The tube itself would have to be tied off, further lessening the odds that Tina could become pregnant.

That season tested Tina in a way I'll never forget. Not only did she already fear her chances were slim because of the endometriosis and the surgery on her uterus, now she had just one functioning fallopian tube, instead of two. In her mind, it felt like the door was closing. And honestly, I thought so too. Hope once tasted, can feel even more painful when it's taken away.

Not long after the heartbreak of losing our baby because of the ectopic pregnancy, the Cleggs got pregnant with their first child.

Tina genuinely rejoiced with Linda. Once again, I saw something in her that still moves me when I think about it. Despite her fresh pain and loss, she showed love. She asked questions. She cared. She celebrated. And then, she would come home and cry. Her crying wasn't loud. It didn't clamor for attention. It was heavy with grief. Tina's heartbroken crying was the kind that says, *Lord, I'm trying to be happy for her...but I'm hurting so much.*

Of course Tina felt envy. She was human. But like Hannah, she refused to let envy turn into bitterness. She refused to let pain make her cruel. She honored God in that struggle, even when it cost her.

"I could be bitter, or I can be better," Tina would say. *"I want to be better."*

When John and Linda found out they were having a baby girl, Tina took Linda to the mall and spent the day with her, shopping and buying baby clothes, despite wrestling with the pain of her own longing.

I still believe with all my heart that those choices mattered. Not because good behavior "earns" a miracle, but because God meets people in surrendered places, like where I was now, listening for His voice in my memories.

Something holy was happening in Tina back then: she was learning how to love others while her own heart was breaking. That is not natural; it's formed, shaped by real love. A love too real to explain, except that it comes from God.

And like Hannah, Tina prayed—fervently, stubbornly, faithfully. She clung to that little paper, reading and re-reading 1 Samuel. We both wavered, even doubted sometimes. But Tina never stopped praying. She believed that if God gave her a child, she would dedicate that child to Him.

Tina pregnant with Marcus, 1992

Even after the ectopic pregnancy and the surgeries, despite the lessened odds, Tina and I kept trying to have a baby. We kept taking pregnancy tests. After so many negative ones, we were afraid to hope. Would this latest one be another heartbreak? We were both stunned when it showed positive. We were too afraid to be cautiously optimistic. How could we survive another blow like the last one?

But a visit to Dr. Pogorski not only confirmed the pregnancy, he said everything looked normal. I remember how we celebrated—like people who had been holding their breath for years and finally exhaled. After five years of trying, God had finally answered our prayers. Over the next months Tina positively glowed with pregnancy. She radiated joy and gratitude through every single moment of carrying a tiny new life within her. She was absolutely delighted to be a mother.

When it was time for our baby to be born, I was right there in the delivery room with Tina, holding her hand. Our hearts overflowed with anticipation through almost twenty-two hours of painstaking labor. We chose not to learn the baby's gender ahead of time; we were eager for that moment of surprise. And when the time came, Dr. Pogorski announced, *"It's a boy!"*

On December 7, 1992 at 11:22 pm, Marcus Grimmie, our firstborn eagerly came into the world a full month early. We were overjoyed! God's miracle of life had happened through us. I felt so proud, exhilarated, and exhausted all at the same time. As soon as Marcus was born the nurse laid him on Tina's chest, but our little family's moment of joy quickly turned to confusion. Almost immediately after snuggling into Tina's arms, Marcus was whisked away. We didn't yet understand what was happening and had no idea that anything was wrong. Overwhelmed, grateful, and stunned that our baby was finally here, we kept saying to each other in disbelief: *We have a son.*

The labor had been long and difficult, but we weren't prepared for what happened next. Worn out from the delivery, Tina was taken to a private room to recover. I held her hand and spoke soothingly as we sat waiting, quietly wondering: *Where was our son?*

Suddenly, the door swung open, and three doctors walked in. Their faces were kind, but grave. They told us that Marcus had experienced difficulty breathing during the long labor and was now being treated in the neonatal intensive care unit. The atmosphere changed. Our happiness turned into a heartfelt plea to God; the kind that rises up when you have nothing to bargain with, nothing to prove, only trust to cling to.

The doctors advised us to try to get some sleep. They assured us that we could see Marcus in the morning.

I barely heard the words. Tina and I stared into each other's faces, a wave of silence crashing over us as the doctors left the room. I dropped to my knees beside the hospital bed. We held each other's hands tightly, and together, we prayed, pouring our hearts out to God. We were still in awe of the miracle we'd just witnessed, but we also feared for our son's life.

Our joy had so quickly turned to uncertainty. We'd gone from elation to a terrifying new kind of love—the kind that trembles at the thought of loss.

My mind went back to what the doctors had told Tina when she was a teenager—that she might never have children because of endometriosis. But here we were, holding onto each other and praying for the life of the baby we had longed for, the precious little boy fighting to breathe just a few rooms away.

Even now, the words of 1 Samuel 1:27 come to mind.

Lord, this is a child born of prayer.

And even in that fear, even before we knew what the outcome would be, I remember Tina and I prayed with a strange confidence that Marcus would be okay. Not because we were strong, but because God had been with us all along. When we had hope, He was there. When we lost hope, He was there. When we were afraid to hope again, His word was with us. He was always there.

At that moment, Tina and I had learned something deep about love. That still, small voice echoed in my mind all these years later.

Love doesn't wait for everything to be perfect. It shows up in the fear, in the prayers whispered through tears, and in the quiet trust that God is near—even when the road takes a turn you never expected.

Sitting outside the condo on Kenwood Drive in Sicklerville, I thanked God for everything that had happened in my life. I thanked Him for my wife and my son and my daughter and our lives together. None of it had been an accident. God had been with us through tears and doubt and waiting. His love held our family together when it felt like everything was falling apart.

Like Tina, I prayed for God to give me the strength to hope when my heart was breaking. I asked Him to help me go on, trusting that no matter what, He'd always be there.

Love for Marcus filled our hearts and home

Our fervent prayers were answered, and Marcus came through the breathing difficulties with flying colors. Tina and I were able to take him home after just a couple of days in the NICU. Before long he was even sleeping through the night. Marcus was a healthy and happy baby boy, and Tina and I couldn't have been more overjoyed.

I left the condo and took the on-ramp from Berlin-Crosskeys Road, nosing the car into light traffic on the Atlantic City Expressway. Before long I'd settled in for the drive back Ocean City, my thoughts lingering in the past.

While she was pregnant, Tina had been really nervous about having a little girl, so when Marcus was born she was relieved that he was a boy. She didn't know if she could love a daughter—whether she would know how to—because her mom hadn't shown her.

About a month after Marcus arrived, we bundled our little family into the car to go visit my parents in West Berlin, a couple of towns over from where we lived in Sicklerville. It was something of a big deal because Tina had been extremely protective of Marcus since those first few days in the hospital. She was almost afraid to take him anywhere. No stores. No church. No places with crowds. Marcus was brand new, the winter air was cold, and Tina's motherly instincts were on high alert.

I half-glanced toward the back seat of the rental and thought about how much Tina's love for our son helped change her mind about having children.

On the way to my parents' that day, Marcus slept contentedly in his little carseat as we drove along Williamstown Road. Tina sat half-turned around in the front passenger seat, her eyes glued to his little face, taking him in with such love and gratitude. My heart warmed at the memory.

Tina's voice echoed in my mind. *"You know what?"* she asked, *"I think we should have another baby. What do you think?"*

Alone in the rental car, I laughed out loud remembering how I'd tried to act nonchalantly, while inside I was anything but calm. It was one of those defining moments you don't appreciate until much later ... a soft-spoken question in a moving car that changed the shape of our lives. Tina's question wasn't about timing. It was about love. Her eyes sparkled with hope and wonder.

While she was pregnant with Marcus, Tina had carried a fear she didn't admit to anyone but me—that she might be like her mom, that maybe she couldn't love her child the way a mother should.

For me, there was never any doubt. I kept telling her what I believed in my heart: *"Tina, you're going to be a great mom."*

I repeated it so often, it became a kind of refrain in our home.

Marcus arrived, and Tina's love for him wasn't small or cautious. It was an explosion that surprised even her. So, when she asked about a second baby, I knew what was underneath. Her real questions reflected her deepest fears.

If I love Marcus this much, is there room enough in me to love another child? And what if it's a girl? What if I become the thing I'm afraid of? What if I'm like my mom?

Then, in June of 1993, another home pregnancy test came up positive. Tina could barely contain her excitement. A visit to Dr. Pogorski confirmed the result, and suddenly we weren't having a hypothetical conversation anymore. It was real. We had a date on the calendar and another baby on the way.

Tina didn't miss a beat. She was amazing with Marcus. She cared for him with the same tenderness and attention as always, even with a new little one growing inside her. Again, we decided to wait until the baby was born to find out its gender. We wanted the surprise of that moment this time, too.

Each checkup assured us that everything looked fine. Dr. Pogorski reminded us that since Marcus had come early, this baby would probably come early—maybe even earlier than Marcus had. He advised us to be watchful, to be ready, because the timeline could shift without warning.

Except, the closer Tina got to her due date, the more "ready" took on a different meaning. And then, the due date came and went. Dr. Pogorski was nearing retirement, and I laughed, remembering how Tina was so done with being pregnant that she was ready to strangle his young assistant, Dr. Arnes. During one visit, only half joking, she grabbed his tie and told him, *"You better induce me!"*

That was Tina–full of love, full of nerves, full of resolve–all at the same time. Absolutely ready to meet the new baby, we watched the calendar with one eye and Tina's body with the other. Every twinge made us wonder. Every cramp gave us pause.

And then, when it was time, it was time.

I can still remember the movement of that day: the urgency underneath ordinary things. The way, one minute we were doing normal life, and then suddenly, we weren't. We were gathering bags and checking the carseat, trying to remember if there was anything we forgot. And all the while the greatest miracle in the world was happening for us again, whether we were ready or not.

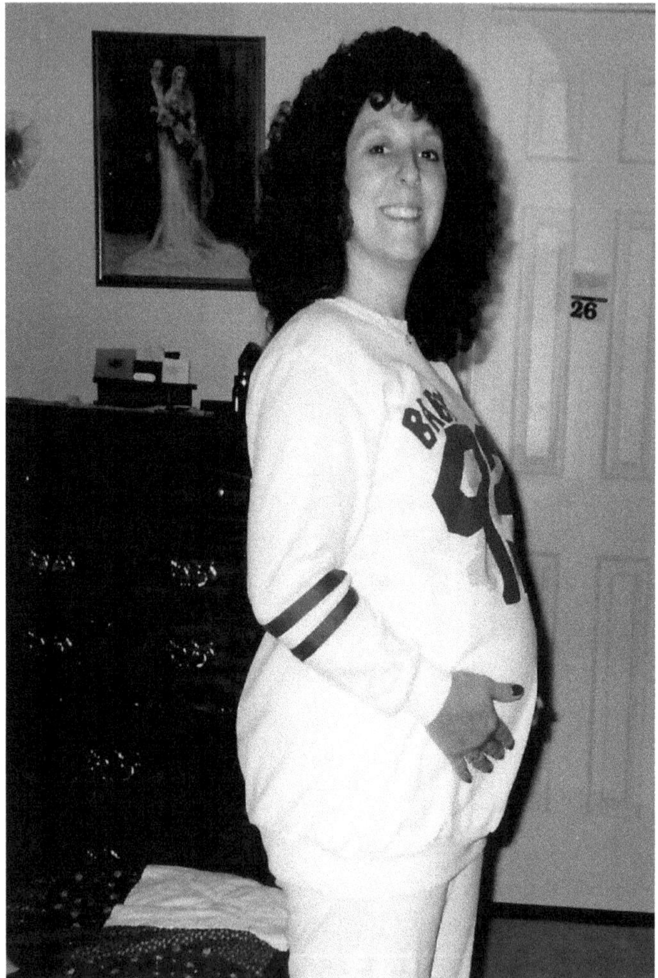

Tina pregnant with Christina, 1993

Tina was focused and determined. She had been fearful early on that she might not love a daughter the way a mother should, that she might repeat the wounds she suffered. But now, at the end of this pregnancy, she looked nothing like fear. She looked resolute. Her face floated in my mind like it was yesterday. She looked like a woman who had discovered that love is not something you ration out with a measuring cup. Love is something God designed to expand.

We settled in at the hospital, and the hours began to stack atop one another. Time passed slowly, marked by nurses coming and going, clipped instructions, and the soft hum of machines. The strange stillness between contractions was punctuated by Tina's grip around my fingers, tightening like she was keeping a promise to break them.

In that stillness I thought about Marcus, likely being cuddled in my mom's arms or bounced on my dad's knee while Tina and I waited for the new baby to be born. How would there be room in our hearts for another baby? I didn't doubt there would be, but our love for Marcus seemed to fill our hearts and the whole house from floor to ceiling.

In an instant, everything in the delivery room shifted from labor to arrival. Voices got sharper and more urgent. Tina pushed, strong and deep. I tried to be steady, tried to be present the best way I knew how. I leaned in close, spoke calmly, and tried not to let my face betray my racing heart.

And then came the cry—that first cry that cuts through the chaos and makes the world brand new.

Time did what it always does in moments like that—it both stopped and flew. One second you're holding your breath, the next you're holding a new little life.

"It's a girl," came the announcement.

A girl.

I saw Tina's face at that moment. Not the face of someone afraid she'd be like her mother, or worried that love might have limits. Hers was a face flooded with the joy of motherhood, just like the first time, overflowing with a love she didn't have to manufacture. I watched something settle in her, something quiet, but permanent. She could love our daughter. She already loved her.

A nurse placed Christina in Tina's arms, with me snuggling in close. Everything changed shape. The room. The future. Our family. I remember looking at our daughter and thinking, *So this is what God does. He doesn't just give you a child. He gives you the capacity to love that child with love you didn't know you had.*

On March 12, 1994 at 10:14 am, our daughter, Christina Victoria Grimmie was born into the world. And Tina was born into a new freedom. God gave me a front-row seat to watch Him answer Tina's fears with love, right there in a hospital room. Love not divided or reduced, but expanded.

We brought Christina home, and Tina poured her whole being into loving our children and me. Her old fears melted away, not because life was easy, life is rarely that; she'd carried the doubt for years: *Would she love her child? Then, could she love another? What if it's a girl?* God answered with a resounding yes.

The woman who once said she never wanted kids was now the heartbeat of our home. Her determination amazed me, especially considering how little sleep we got in those early years. Christina didn't embrace sleep quite as readily as Marcus had.

Tina loved deeply and parented with passion. She wasn't the kind of mom who was just going through the motions —she was the all-in, fierce-protector, bend-down-and-look-you-in-the-eyes kind. She had instincts I didn't even know existed.

With Marcus, she learned to navigate the world of toddler boy energy—full of movement, curiosity, and endless questions. And Christina brought out a softness, a tenderness that came from a different place, one that had been so wounded in her as a little girl.

"Holding Christina feels like healing part of my own heart." Tina had said those words countless times.

Tina thrived in giving our kids what she had always longed for: love, stability, affection, boundaries wrapped in grace, and a fierce, steady presence. She was intentional. She was involved. She was the one who knelt beside the crib and prayed. She showed up with handmade Valentines for class parties and stayed up late making sure birthday parties were just right—even if it meant going overboard on decorations.

And our house? It pulsed with life because of her. Laughter echoed off the walls. I often said I married Tina because she laughed at my jokes. Music played, and we danced. There was a rhythm to our days—a rhythm Tina created out of love, and sometimes, sheer willpower.

For Tina, the best part of the day often came after the sun had set and the house began to slow down. Dinner was done. Dishes were in the sink. Pajamas were on. The chaotic energy of young kids started to soften into something calmer, more tender. It was bedtime—and Tina made it a sacred routine.

She didn't just put our kids to bed—she tucked them in. There was a difference. Every night had its rhythm: teeth brushed, stories read, lights dimmed just right. But what made it special was how personal she made it for each child.

She loved just having conversations with Marcus. She'd sit on the edge of his bed and talk with him about whatever was on his mind—dinosaurs, dreams, the things he noticed at school. She listened. She really listened. And she gave him room to be curious, to process, to wonder.

With Christina, it was music. Sometimes Tina would sing softly as she brushed Christina's hair—those little lullabies that lived somewhere between a whisper and a prayer. Other nights, Christina would ask for her favorite: *"Sing, Mommy...sing that one again."* And Tina, tired as she might've been, would smile and start right in.

I spotted the exit for the Garden State Parkway and smiled, remembering the laughter. There were tickle fights and last-minute sips of water and the occasional *"just one more story."* Tina never saw any of it as a chore. Even so, I relished nights when I could be home early to act out the story of David and Goliath at bedtime. Seeing Tina be with the kids so lovingly and passionately inspired me to want to be part of that, to share in those special moments. Her life and her actions were shaping me, especially those nights when the cancer treatments wore her down, tiring her out and making more than a prayer and a kiss goodnight for the kids too hard for her. I felt God energizing me to be better for Tina and for my family.

For Tina, motherhood was her ministry. Her love for our children came through in the smallest things: the way she straightened their blankets, the way she prayed over them before turning out the light, the way she lingered at the door just a few seconds longer, her words barely more than a whisper, meant just for them.

"I love you more than you know."

Sometimes I'd stand outside in the hallway and just watch, taking it all in and marveling at the woman who once feared motherhood walking so confidently in it. The way God had softened and shaped her was like witnessing a miracle happening in slow motion. I didn't know then how much I'd cherish those ordinary nights. I didn't know how many times in the future I'd return to those memories—not to escape, but to remind myself that even in the simplest routines, there was a holy kind of love at work.

Some women turn out to be good moms because of the example their mothers set for them. Tina didn't have that, and yet she was an incredible mother. She loved Marcus and Christina the way she'd wanted to be loved, the way she believed God loved all of us—lavishly and with no reservations.

Tina was fully immersed in being mom to Marcus and Christina—and she thrived in it in a way that surprised even her. I believe God allowed her to walk in her calling as a mother with her whole heart so that when the trials came, there would already be deep roots of love and legacy in place.

The first sign of change came like an ominous bump in the road of our family's happy routine.

Chapter Ten

The Call That Changed Everything

A little over a year after Christina was born, Tina went in for a routine appointment with her gynecologist Dr. Pogorski. She wasn't experiencing anything out of the ordinary. She had recovered well from the pregnancy and was back in her usual routines. On the surface, everything seemed fine.

But that afternoon, returning from her appointment, she walked through the door of our condo with a different look on her face.

"I need to get a mammogram," she said.

There wasn't a dramatic moment—just a quiet statement. Dr. Pogorski was preparing to retire after decades in gynecology. We trusted him. He hadn't sounded panicked; he'd just noticed a soft lump that had been there for a few weeks now seemed hard. But Tina wasn't yet 36, and the test he ordered wasn't standard for someone her age unless there was cause for concern.

Whatever trepidation she might have felt, she scheduled the appointment without hesitation. That was Tina—when it came to her health, she didn't procrastinate. She was proactive. Disciplined. Brave. What none of us knew then was that this simple appointment would be the beginning of a road we never imagined we'd have to walk. It would be the first ripple in what would become a tidal wave of faith, fear, surrender, and ultimately a test of our commitment to each other.

Looking back now, it's clear—God was already preparing us. Even in that quiet moment, standing in our home with Christina just a baby, and Marcus a toddler,

God was there. And Tina, without knowing it, was stepping into one of the most courageous seasons of her life.

The mammogram appointment came and went that day. Nothing dramatic. Nothing alarming. Afterward Tina walked through the door like she always did—organized, composed, already thinking about what came next in the day.

But then, the phone rang that night. It was the doctor from the radiologist's office who had reviewed the images from Tina's mammogram. He said she needed to call her doctor immediately and arrange to come in for an office visit first thing the next morning. No waiting. No vague reassurances. Just a direct statement. The mammogram had revealed a lump that required a biopsy. Urgently.

Tina hung up the phone, her face pale. The conversation was brief, but it shook her. I could see it in her eyes—her mind was already racing.

For Tina, the swiftness of the call was jarring. It wasn't just the news—it was how it came. The tone. The urgency. It wasn't delivered with gentleness or care, and that upset and angered her. The call had landed like a hammer blow in the stillness of our home. One minute we were managing a normal day; the next, we were staring into the unknown.

That night, we didn't say much. We sat together, trying to keep things normal for the kids, but inside, everything felt different. There's a kind of silence that settles in when fear is present—a silence that feels heavier than words.

Tina wasn't someone who ran from hard things. But I knew her well enough to recognize the fear behind her eyes. She had lived through years of health struggles already. And now this.

It's amazing how a single moment can change everything. One phone call. One sentence. One urgent request from an unknown radiologist to *"See your doctor tomorrow morning."*

That night, we prayed, even though we didn't have the words. We were experiencing what steady love looks like—not in grand gestures or powerful answers, but in the quiet decision to stay close, to trust God in the not-yet, and to face whatever was coming—together.

After the biopsy, my sister recommended a surgeon she trusted—Dr. Butler.

She called him *the singing surgeon.* I'm not kidding. He was known for humming or even softly singing to his patients, especially before surgery. It was a little unusual, but he came highly recommended. At the time, we welcomed anything that brought a human touch into what had quickly become a very clinical, intimidating world. We scheduled an appointment with Dr. Butler to get the biopsy results.

Tina and I sat side by side in his office, waiting. We were quiet. Steadying ourselves. Hoping. Praying. Dreading. All at once.

Dr. Butler walked in, his presence calm as he gently greeted us. He sat down across from us and got straight to the point.

"I have the results," he said. *"It's breast cancer."*

The room kept spinning, even as the world stopped.

I'm sure he kept talking after that. I'm sure he explained that it was *Ductal Carcinoma In Situ—or DCIS*—a very early, non-invasive form of breast cancer. He probably told us that it hadn't spread, that it was Stage 0, that it was highly treatable with chemotherapy and had a very high survival rate.

But none of that mattered in that moment. All we heard were the words *breast cancer.*

Tina looked at me, and I looked at her—we both knew: our lives had just changed. Whether it was Stage 0 or Stage 4, the word *cancer* had entered our story. It had found its way into our marriage, into our family, into the precious, messy, beautiful life we were building with our two kids.

We were devastated.

Even the kindest voice and calmest explanation couldn't soften the blow. That day, the "singing surgeon" wasn't singing. And neither were we.

It's strange how your whole world can narrow into one word.

Cancer.

Not the full story. Not the prognosis. Just the word.

Even when the doctors use words like early or treatable, your brain doesn't hear that first. Your heart doesn't hold onto that right away. You hear fear. You feel loss. You grieve what hasn't even happened yet.

But at that moment—frozen in the doctor's office, holding Tina's hand—what I remember most wasn't the clinical terms or percentages. It was her.

And it was the way we silently decided—somehow, words weren't necessary—that we would walk through this together, whatever it meant.

I felt the realization, full and strong, just like I had sitting next to Tina while the singing surgeon's words seemed to turn the love song of our lives into a dirge. Love doesn't always understand. It doesn't always feel strong. But it stays, even when we try to run away.

Tina had always been meticulous about her health—especially after being diagnosed with endometriosis as a teenager. Because of that she learned early on to take her body seriously, to keep track of symptoms, to never ignore her doctor's advice, and especially to be her own best advocate. She was even more determined to care for her body because of the chemotherapy. She followed her doctor's orders, drank lots of water and tried to make healthier food choices. Tina was not passive in the process. She was fighting with the same determination she gave everything she did, including, caring for Marcus and Christina in the midst of battling cancer.

That first round of chemo was physically rough on Tina, but beyond that, the cancer began to take an emotional and spiritual toll. Tina always put on a good face, but I could tell she was languishing inside. She refused to have anything to do with anyone she thought might have cancer. It was as though she could sense the presence of the disease, even without the tell-tale signs of scarves or wigs hiding heads gone bald from chemo treatments. When pressed she would engage briefly, then quickly back away—maybe in denial that she, too, was facing cancer.

Chapter Eleven

Lessons Learned

After Tina's initial diagnosis she started chemotherapy right away.

I navigated the A.C. Expressway and made my way onto the Garden State Parkway, then took the Ninth Street Bridge into Ocean City. I arrived at the condo, parked, shut off the engine and went inside.

Back then, when we first found out about Tina's cancer, we were turning a corner financially, but I was working a lot of overtime at Verizon and getting home late most nights. Some weeks I logged fifty-five hours. My mom and dad helped us enormously during that season. My mother would come over and help watch the kids while I was at work. My dad, who had retired a couple of years before Marcus was born, would often take Tina to her treatments. That was no small thing. Those appointments were heavy, physically and emotionally. I've often looked back with deep gratitude that Tina didn't have to go through all of them alone.

Physically Tina was coping, but emotionally and spiritually, she shut down. I'd come home from work and sometimes she'd have her Bible open, but she wasn't really reading anything. Even attending church had started to become a strain. We continued going on Sundays, but Tina was just numb.

Marcus and Christina were only two and three years old in 1995, too young to understand the weight their mother was carrying. To them, she was still Mom. Still the one they reached for, the one who knew what they needed. She was still the heart of our home, making life as normal for them as she could, insisting they did things like play dates and Sunday school. Life didn't pause just because our world had been shaken.

Tina and Christina, Niagara Falls

Each Sunday morning, I'd take both kids down to their classrooms while Tina went into the sanctuary for the service. Marcus to kindergarten. Christina to the nursery. Marcus fit in easily with the other Sunday school kids. Bright and social, he could always find his way in a new environment. Christina, on the other hand, was struggling.

At that age, she had intense separation anxiety, especially being apart from Tina. Leaving either of us was hard for her, but being apart from her mom? That was unbearable. She cried every Sunday. I'd usually linger by the nursery door for a few moments, listening. If Christina's crying stopped, even for just a minute or two, I'd slip upstairs to the sanctuary to catch the sermon.

One particular Sunday morning, the pattern seemed to hold. I heard her calm down after a little while and headed up the stairs, hoping the worst was over.

But as the sermon began to wrap up, something nudged me to head down to the nursery early. As I descended the stairs, I heard it—loud, breathless crying. Christina. Her cries were so intense she was gasping between sobs. My heart dropped. This was not the sound of a child who had just started crying.

I rushed to the nursery and before I even reached the door I saw her through the window. She was slumped in a corner, her face streaked with snot and tears, her little body trembling with sobs. And in the adjacent room, two nursery attendants sat, chatting casually, oblivious to Christina's heart-rending cries.

The pressure behind my eyes felt as though my head would explode. I felt my temperature go up a couple of degrees.

Had Tina been there, she would've blown the doors off the hinges.

I pushed through the doorway. The two women jumped, startled by my abrupt entrance. I shot them a look I knew said everything I was thinking.

I went straight to Christina. She melted into my arms, her little face hot and clammy from the crying, her eyes red and swollen. She clung to me like she was afraid I might leave her again.

I turned to the women and asked—too angry to be subtle.

"What's going on? Why didn't you check on her?" I asked.

"We were letting her cry it out," one of them answered.

We exchanged a few more words as I hugged my daughter closer, gathered her things and left.

Tina came out of the service and with one look at Christina's face–flushed, streaked with tears, little hiccoughs interrupting her breathing–her hackles rose. She demanded to know what had happened. I briefly explained as we grabbed Marcus from kindergarten class and headed toward the parking lot.

I waited until we were safely in the car to tell her everything. Tina was furious, nearly trembling with rage. She was quiet—at first. I could tell she was biting her tongue to keep from upsetting the kids, containing the explosion building inside her. But when we got home, her fury spilled over, and understandably so.

I was close with one of the pastors at church, so I called to tell him what happened. He picked up and asked his wife to listen in.

I intended to calmly communicate the issue and address it directly and respectfully. But as I began explaining, Tina—still burning with emotion—cut in and began expressing her anger.

And just like that, the focus shifted. Her righteous frustration came out sharp and loud—and suddenly, instead of being about our concerns with the nursery staff, the conversation became about Tina's reaction. She realized that after I hung up. And to her credit, she didn't double down.

Years later, even sitting alone in Ocean City where we'd spent so much time talking about our relationship, I was still amazed by Tina in moments like that. Her emotions could ignite like wildfire, especially when it came to protecting our kids. But just as quickly, she could humble herself. She knew when her reaction had become a distraction. And she always had the heart to acknowledge it and turn back toward grace.

One of her deepest fears early in our marriage was that I might be too passive, that when hard things came she would be forced to take charge. She could do that, of course, but it was never what she wanted. She longed to know that I would be her knight in shining armor, her protector.

But the nursery experience taught us something about each other.

I saw once again how fiercely Tina loved our children—how deeply she felt injustice and how quick she was to stand up against it. The same passion that made her fiery could just as quickly turn into humility when the Holy Spirit nudged her heart.

And I think she saw in me a quiet steadiness that God had been shaping over time—a steadiness not only to handle the moment but to handle her, with grace. I learned to anticipate situations that might set Tina off, and to step in first. I would react quickly, voicing my own displeasure and taking a stand before the moment had a chance to fully escalate for her. My response was usually not as intense as hers might have been. But once she saw that I was sensitive to her concern and was willing to act on her behalf she could let go of the need to charge ahead to protect herself or our family. It was as though my response gave her permission to let go. She could trust that I would help guard what was right in the life we were building together.

We began regularly praying for wisdom and discernment about who would watch over our children in our stead. That awareness would be critical as the kids entered the spotlight, especially as Christina gained popularity on YouTube.

I came to see how important that was to her. Had I not been willing to stand up for her, or had I not had the strength to push back when needed, Tina would have taken over by necessity. And in time, I believe she would have resented me for making her bear a weight she never wanted to carry alone–whether that was raising a family, or battling cancer, or losing our daughter.

Our marriage was not perfect. We didn't always get it right. But by growing through each other's imperfections, offering grace in real-time, and recognizing that even when we're off balance, God is teaching us, shaping us, and holding us, we learned something of what it feels like to be loved by God. These memories brought me peace; reliving them felt revitalizing and therapeutic–even here without Tina, without Christina. God had not left me. He would keep holding me. I went to the bedroom and got ready for bed. Content with my thoughts, I drifted off to sleep.

***

I woke up early, thoughts still lingering from the night before. God had indeed been with me and kept me through the years. I made my way to the kitchen, where my Bible and the 100-day goal journal lay open on the table. The brutal cold had crept into the condo overnight. I hurried across the icy tiles and reached for the thermostat. The start of another chilly day came to mind.

It had started like a typical morning. I was the first one up. The house was cold from the night air, so I padded downstairs to turn up the thermostat. Nothing unusual. But as I climbed the stairs back to our bedroom, something shifted. I felt a strange kink in my neck—something off, but not alarming. By the time I reached my side of the bed, a sudden wave of intense chest pain hit me. Sharp. Crushing. I lay down, trying to make sense of it.

"Tina," I said, trying to stay calm. *"Something's wrong. Maybe a heart attack."*

The pain escalated fast. Tina didn't hesitate—she grabbed the phone and called for help. Within minutes, paramedics arrived and strapped me into a stair chair to carry me down. As we reached the bottom of the steps, things began to blur. I started to black out. Then the cold outdoor air slapped my face, and I became faintly aware I was being loaded into the ambulance.

Neighbors showed up just in time to watch the kids so Tina could follow in the car. As the ambulance pulled away, I sat there on the stretcher, and something extraordinary happened.

A peace I cannot describe came over me.

Not just calm—*peace.* Deep, settling, sacred.

I remember thinking, *This might be it. I think I'm about to die.*

And strangely, I wasn't afraid.

This is what I had talked about so many times while sharing the Gospel—asking people: *"Do you know where you're going when you die?"* They'd look at me like I was odd, maybe even morbid. But I wasn't talking about fear—I was talking about certainty. Assurance.

Now, here I was, *living* the question I had asked so many others.

And I was ready. In fact, I felt excited. If this was the end, I would be with Jesus. No fear. Just overwhelming peace and the presence of God pressing in on every side. I didn't know it then, but I was experiencing God in the middle of an ambulance ride—on the edge of life and death.

When we got to the hospital, they wheeled me into the ER. I was trying to breathe but my chest felt like a cement block. And suddenly—*there she was.*

Tina flew into the room like a hurricane.

She leaned over me, tears in her eyes. *"Bud, I'm right here. I love you. I'm not leaving your side."*

Through the fog of pain, I smiled weakly. *"T, I'm so glad you're here. I need you to know, I'm okay. I'm at peace. I'm ready to die. Don't feel bad."*

That's when Tina flipped.

She started yelling—through her tears, of course. *"You're NOT going anywhere! What are you talking about? You can't go now!"*

Only Tina could love me enough to yell at me for being at peace with God on the verge of death. Even in a crisis, her fierce love came out swinging.

Just then, a doctor came in, gently guiding Tina out of the way as nurses swarmed in to prep me for surgery. One of them came in holding an X-ray, which she handed to the doctor. Tina, not quite done with her moment, *grabbed the X-ray right out of the doctor's hands*, held it up to the light, and stared at it like she knew what she was doing.

The doctor, looking amused and slightly baffled, asked, *"Do you know what you're looking at?"*

Tina exhaled and admitted, *"No,"* she said and handed it back.

The doctor kindly asked her to wait outside as they wheeled me off to the OR.

The diagnosis: a spontaneous pneumothorax. My right lung had collapsed—just like that. Apparently, this kind of thing is relatively common in tall, thin men. Lucky me.

But in the operating room, long before I knew the name of what was wrong with me, I had already experienced something greater than medicine could explain. I had encountered the presence of God. That ambulance ride became a spiritual marker in my life. Interestingly enough, I had been leading an *Experiencing God* study with a group of college and career-age young adults at Bethel around the time my lung collapsed. The hospital allowed them all to come to my room for study time while I was recovering.

I didn't ask for a divine encounter that day. I didn't orchestrate it with music or a Bible in hand. But *He was there*. In the pain. In the unknown. In the moment between fear and surrender, God met me.

I had shared the message of salvation with others so many times—promising that those who trust in Jesus don't have to fear death. That to be absent from the body is to be present with the Lord. And on that morning, as my lung collapsed and my body gave out, I got to *experience* that message in real time.

Peace isn't the absence of suffering. It's the undeniable presence of God *within* it.

I smiled at the memory. Tina experienced God that day, too—in her own way. Her faith was fierce, her love louder than fear, and her instinct to fight for me never wavered.

My collapsed lung had been another reminder of God's love in our lives—not just in theology or moments of joy, but right there in the chaos of the ER, in between X-rays, and through Tina's shouted protests of, *"You're not going anywhere!"*

She was right. I wasn't going anywhere. Not yet. But even if I had, I would've gone in peace.

I felt a similar peace enveloping me, now, as I watched the sunrise through the kitchen window of the condo. The God who had spared my life and healed my collapsed lung was healing my broken heart.

I hadn't re-stocked the fridge or pantry since I'd arrived. I took a quick inventory and made a list of things to grab from the grocery store, including something to bring to my sister Carole's for Christmas dinner in a few days.

Christmas had been Tina's favorite time of year ever since she was a little girl. As a wife and mom creating her own family traditions, she'd spend hours decorating the house and cooking a huge turkey dinner with all the trimmings. And she'd set Grandmom Milos' Romanian baklava and kifla center-stage for dessert.

Christmas was Tina's favorite time of year, even as a little girl

I loved to stand in the kitchen doorway and just watch while Tina busied about seasoning and stirring, mixing and tasting. She'd sing and dance around our little kitchen as though it were the happiest place in the world. When she saw me, she'd toss her chestnut brown hair and flash me a smile that made my heart skip a beat.

We'd fallen in love with the people at Bethel Church through the Christian school and prayer ministry. *"I was like a dried up sponge, and they were pouring water on me,"* Tina said many times of the people we met there. Each year, members assemble into a living Christmas tree. Row upon row of people stood on lighted bleachers singing Christmas carols accompanied by a live orchestra. I remember the Christmas when Tina stood in the special place at the very top of the tree. She was so excited. She invited everyone to the concert, even her nurses from Penn Oncology.

I sat in the audience, watching her sing, her face as radiant as the twinkling star behind her head. She sang with so much joy; if it weren't for the tell-tale scarf wrapped too flat against her head, you'd never know that all her hair had fallen out with the second round of chemo. She smiled from the top of the tree, and as always, my heart skipped a beat.

Tina's smile was as bright as the star on top of the tree

Just as fiercely as she stood between me and death the day my lung collapsed, Tina was determined to shield Marcus and Christina from the impact of her cancer diagnosis. We were learning that suffering was not the end of the story, though it often felt like the whole story while we were in it. Tina didn't want to waste time being sick or sad. She feared that Marcus and Christina wouldn't remember her if she died while they were little, so she poured herself into every aspect of their lives. Her passion and dedication to our kids was infectious.

We had moved out of our condo in Sicklerville and were living in our first house in Atco, not far from where I grew up. We were attending Bethel Church when I first sensed something I couldn't quite explain—something deeper than just a passing thought. It was a distinct leading in my spirit, one that didn't feel like my own idea. It felt like God's.

I told Tina about it. *"I think I'm supposed to help Cindy with the Sunday school program at the Family Center."*

Tina and I were still relatively new to Bethel at the time, and we both believed God had led us there. There were nearly fifty kids in kindergarten through sixth grade with just one volunteer leader, Cindy, who read stories and supervised games while the parents were in Sunday school. Me volunteering wasn't a crazy idea—our own kids were in those grades. Maybe God was nudging me to spend more intentional time with my children. We were doing better financially after being upside down on our house, but I was still working a lot of overtime and missing tucking the kids in with Tina. The weight of being present—not just providing—was pressing on my heart. So, I called Cindy. She was thrilled.

"We don't get a lot of volunteers for story and game time," she said. *"It would be a huge help."*

Sunday school for children was held across the street in the gym where there was plenty of space, and the Christian school classrooms lined the hallway. Parents would drop their kids off at various times throughout the morning during Bible study and worship services. The kids would be with Cindy for story and game time, then split up into age-based classrooms with different teachers. I would help with "crowd control" during the story lesson and then assist the teachers during classes. Each week, we'd pull out the bleachers for nearly fifty kids to gather for a Bible lesson. Afterward, we would walk them to classrooms just down the hallway. I got to know the kids, and I watched my own children light up during those mornings. I began to see firsthand the impact of that simple investment in their lives.

Several months went by, and then one morning, Cindy pulled me aside to tell me that she and her husband felt called to leave Bethel to attend another church. My heart sank a little, but I understood.

That morning, she made the announcement to the kids. An audible groan rippled through the group. You could see it in their faces—they loved Cindy. They were going to miss her. As parents arrived she explained that Sunday school was on pause until further notice because she was leaving, and there was no one to replace her. The church would follow up when a new plan was in place.

As I stood there, watching the disappointment settle over the kids and confusion grow among the parents, I felt that same stirring in my spirit again. It wasn't a voice. It wasn't a dramatic moment. It was just there—a quiet, confident nudge: *Do this. Step in. Keep it going for the kids. Fill in the gap.*

So I went back to Cindy and said, *"I'd like to help. I can fill in for the time being—at least keep storytime going. The classes already have teachers in place. We can do this."*

I spoke to the pastors about what I felt in my heart, and before I knew it—without applying or campaigning or planning for it—I was appointed the new Children's Sunday School Administrator.

There are times when God moves through burning bushes or blinding lights. And then there are times like this, when He simply nudges—gently, quietly, but unmistakably.

I didn't set out to lead a children's ministry. I just wanted to be faithful. I wanted to be present with my kids. I wanted to support someone who was doing good work. But God used that obedience to invite me into something deeper with a whisper, a prompting. A "yes" that didn't make sense at the start but changed lives—including mine.

Small things done in faith have a way of becoming sacred. I think back now on those memories and treasure them. That gym full of kids, the laughter and energy, the stories and snack times and memory verses. I think about my own kids watching me serve. I think about Tina, always supporting, even when it stretched us. Our lives were made for more than just us. Our lives had purpose, even in doing small things like helping out with Sunday school.

With Christina's death, and now Tina's, God hadn't whispered His invitation for me to go deeper. He had roared it so loudly I thought I'd lose my mind. And yet, in the heartbreak He was still extending an invitation.

Chapter Twelve

Experiencing God

I sat at the table in the condo, staring absently at my grocery list. I thought about the intensity of God calling us to a deeper relationship with Him through Tina's first diagnosis in 1995, and how five years later even that was amplified. She had endured what she called being poked and prodded more times than she could count. Her normal rhythm had become routine trips to Quest Diagnostics, regular blood draws, and the always-anxious wait for results.

At first, the tests were every few weeks. Then, once a month. Then every few months. Finally, after four years of hearing "no signs of active cancer," the doctors said we could come back in six months. For a while, we lived in the strange tension of guarded peace, grateful for the word *unremarkable* that kept showing up on her reports.

Then came the call. For the first time in five years, Tina's tumor markers were elevated. She was devastated. The word we had dreaded for years had returned.

Tina immediately reached out to our trusted family doctor, who had walked closely with us through her earlier battle. He calmly reassured her: *"Tumor markers are just indicators, not a diagnosis. Stay calm. Be patient,"* he said.

But now, her fears of the cancer returning that had haunted her dreams for five years loomed large– threatening. And Tina was terrified.

At the same time, my good friend Bill—a pastor at a local Calvary Chapel—invited me to a men's retreat at Sandy Cove in Maryland. I told him, *"I can't leave Tina right now—not for a whole weekend. Maybe another time."*

But when I mentioned it to Tina, she surprised me.

"You should go," she said. *"It'll be good for you. I'll feel better knowing you're with other godly men."*

That was *so* unlike Tina at that stage of our life. In the early years of our marriage, she never wanted us to be apart—especially during something like this. But years later, she told me the truth: *"I was so afraid of the cancer coming back, and I didn't want to cry in front of you. I held it in while you were there. I knew you would keep trying to comfort me, but I wanted to cry and not be consoled. So, while you were gone I cried myself to sleep every night."*

Marcus and Christina were around nine and seven years old at the time. Tina reassured me she'd be fine Friday and Saturday. I'd be back early Sunday. After talking it through, I agreed to go.

That Friday, I met Bill at his house and climbed into a seven-passenger van with him and four other guys. On the drive, they kept talking about someone named "Blackaby." Quotes. Stories. Lives changed.

Finally, I interrupted. *"Alright, who is this Blackaby guy you're all yappin' about?"*

They laughed. Bill explained that Henry Blackaby wrote a study called *Experiencing God*, and how their church had gone through it together. Lives were changing. People were finally seeing God at work—not just hearing sermons, but encountering Him personally.

I was skeptical but curious.

Bill reached under his seat and pulled out a copy of the *Experiencing God* workbook. *"We had one extra from the church study,"* he said. *"You can have it."*

I thanked him, took the book, and tucked it away.

The weekend was powerful. Speakers like Joe Focht and Gayle Erwin poured truth and encouragement into us. I was fed spiritually, challenged, and deeply moved—but I never opened the workbook. There was basketball, swimming, lots of good food—and always, the looming possibility of Tina again needing chemo. My heart and ears were wide open that weekend.

When I returned home Sunday, Tina greeted me with a tired smile. She said the kids had been great and that she'd had a quiet weekend. She loved those times so much, just being home with the kids. Just being their mom. I told her about the retreat, and we both felt strengthened—if only slightly—for the road ahead.

The next morning, I grabbed the *Experiencing God* book and took it with me to work. I was doing a job off Black Horse Pike in Monroe Township with two coworkers. During lunch, I drove to a nearby phone cross box, parked, and opened my brown bag.

While I ate, I flipped through the workbook. It was a 12-week study. The goal was simple: read a short section each day, answer a few questions and reflect. Then share your answers in a group. I didn't plan on joining a group—but something told me to read it anyway.

I opened the workbook to Week 1, Day 1. The first paragraph stopped me cold.

"Jesus said, '*This is eternal life: that they may know You, the only true God, and Jesus Christ, whom You have sent*'" (John 17:3).

Wait—*this* is eternal life? Not just living forever? Not just escaping hell?

Jesus was saying that eternal life was *knowing* the Father and the Son. Not just believing *in* Him, but truly *knowing* Him. It hit me like a ton of bricks. I had been reading and studying my Bible for years. I thought I knew. But this felt new. Fresh. Alive.

As I sat there thinking about it—asking God what this meant for me, for Tina—my beeper suddenly went off.

All 9's. Our family's code for, "*Call immediately.*"

I connected to our company line at the cross box and dialed home.

Tina answered. Her voice was quiet, steady.

"Bud, you need to come home."

I tensed, waiting for what she'd say next.

"The cancer is back. And it's really bad."

I closed the workbook and drove back to the job site. *"I've got to leave,"* I said. *"Tina needs me."*

The testing confirmed our worst fears. The breast cancer had metastasized. It was now in her liver, her lungs, and what scared Tina most—in her bones. It wasn't liver cancer or bone cancer—it was breast cancer that had spread. And it wasn't going away.

I didn't plan to meet with God that Monday. I didn't plan to start a new study. I didn't even know who Henry Blackaby was. But God had already planned that moment. Just as He had been guiding Tina and me through every test, every doctor visit, and every terrifying unknown—He had also prepared a word for me at the exact moment I would need it most.

Eternal life is knowing him.

Not just surviving. Not just managing a crisis. But leaning into a relationship with the only One strong enough to carry us through it. But how do we do that? When everything around us feels unstable, God is already there—present in the retreat, in the lunch break, in the fear, in the love that never leaves; but how do we develop an intimate, love relationship with the Creator of the universe? In my experience, sermons often teach what we should or shouldn't do, the whys and why nots–but the "how" is often overlooked.

Tina and I prayed through the night and slept little. The next morning we sat in the oncologist's office hearing about chemotherapy options. Then we talked with my sister, Carole, who had been a nurse for more than 20 years. *"Go over the bridge,"* she said, which meant go to the University of Penn in Philadelphia. We followed her advice and made an appointment with Dr. Angela Demichelle, a top oncologist at Penn.

Tina explained to Dr. Demichelle that she had a persistent cough that worsened when she lay down. After the examination and some imaging, the doctor told us they had to admit Tina immediately into the hospital. In the next few moments they were rushing her into surgery. There was so much fluid around Tina's heart that they had to perform a pericardial window to drain it in order to save her life.

When she had recovered enough from the pericardial window surgery, Tina began her second round of chemotherapy. Though the prognosis wasn't good, her doctors were cautiously hopeful that she might respond well to this treatment. But for Tina, hope was buried under fear. She had dreaded this moment for years, and now it had come.

That day, she lay in a hospital bed, quiet and downcast. The IV line was already in place, delivering what they called medicine—but what for Tina felt like poison. Nevertheless, it was poison that we prayed would kill the cancer, while fully knowing it would also ravage her body.

This was the very thing she had feared most—confirmation that the cancer had returned, and going through chemo all over again. But it wasn't just her body that felt broken. For the last five years, Tina had been quietly running from God. She still went to church, still showed up—but her heart had grown distant. Her Bible sat mostly unopened. Her prayers faded. She was quiet more often, yet still functioning as super mom for two children under three years old. She was sagging under the weight of the burden of the cancer returning.

Around that time, Sarah Mittelman, a friend of ours from Bethel, was teaching through the book, *Hinds' Feet on High Places* by Hannah Hurnard in adult Bible study at church. It's an allegory where the main character, Much-Afraid journeys from being crippled and fearful to the High Places on a quest for the new name and body promised by her Shepherd. Sarah was encouraged by the story and gave a copy of the book to Tina.

After a week or so I asked Tina if she'd read the book and what she thought.

"Yeah, you'd like it," she said. *"It's good."*

But then she clammed up even more.

I mentioned Tina's reaction to Sarah and said I'd like to read the book.

"You'll love it," she said. *"There's so much depth to it. I will say that not too many guys read it, though."*

I did read the book and absolutely loved it. I was so excited to talk to Tina about it, but she didn't share my enthusiasm, at all. It turns out that the book had frightened her. She thought in despair, *"I have to die to have hinds' feet on high places."*

I was stunned. I hurt for her. My poor Boo.

"T, did you read the preface?" I asked.

"What?" She had no idea why that would matter.

I read the preface aloud to her, explaining that the hinds' feet represented the sure-footedness we could trust God to give us in the high places—the dangerous, scary circumstances of life, like being on the edge of a cliff.

"So, the hinds' feet on high places are for us here and now as God's children?" she repeated, realization dawning on her face.

"Yes, sweetheart," I said, gathering my precious wife into my arms. *"Transforming even the worst circumstances for God's glory and a closer love relationship with Him is meant for now, not after we die,"* I said, *"if we follow the path He's chosen for us."*

Suddenly it dawned on me. Tina and I had both had pivotal revelations about what it meant to have a love relationship with God around the time the cancer returned.

"Eternal life is knowing him."

"...the hinds' feet and high places are for us here and now as God's children..."

Those revelations spoke to me as I thought about how, a few weeks later, I sat at the foot of Tina's hospital bed, the *Experiencing God* workbook lying open in my lap. I had just started it a few days earlier and was wrestling through it, trying to make sense of what "experiencing God" really looked like in the middle of something like this. Watching her lying there, pale and silent, I felt helpless. I prayed quietly, asking God for anything—guidance, comfort, hope. I believed He loved us. I believed He was real. But at that moment, all I could ask was: *Why, God? Why Tina—again?*

She stirred, pulled the blanket aside, and slid her feet to the floor. *"I need to use the restroom,"* she said softly. She grabbed the IV pole—the bag of chemo still dripping—and slowly shuffled across the room.

What I didn't know then was that Tina wasn't just headed to the restroom. She was headed to surrender. I could still see her face, hear her voice as she told me what had happened while I sat waiting for her to come out of the restroom.

"Inside the bathroom, I just dropped to my knees," she said. *"I couldn't take it anymore. The weight of five years of fear, of distant prayers, of pain buried deep, it just all came pouring out. I couldn't stop crying. I felt like a turtle without a shell.*

"I said to Him, 'God, I can't do this. I need You now—more than I ever have. Please, Lord, help me. I need to know You're with me. I can't do this alone anymore. Please, show me You're with me. Somehow. Please.'

"I stayed there, praying with everything I had. Then, I got up and made my way back to the bed. I didn't feel any different. No lightning bolt. No voice from heaven. Just the same quiet fear. You were sitting at the end of the bed, your Experiencing God workbook half-hanging off your lap. I got back in the bed and pulled the covers up, wondering if God had heard me—or if He even cared."

Tina lay in bed, her eyes closed, breathing soft. I just looked at her, prayed for her, and held her hand. Moments later, there was a knock at the hospital door.

In walked the nurse, followed closely by a woman in a business suit. The nurse explained that the woman worked for the company that made the chemo machines. She was there for "*Just a routine check,*" that would only take a few minutes.

But then something unexpected happened. As the nurse turned to adjust the machine, she noticed the Bible lying on the edge of Tina's bed. She stopped. Then, pointing her finger directly at Tina, she asked—in a voice loud and full of conviction: "*Is that your Bible?*"

Tina nodded, unsure what to say.

Without hesitation, the nurse declared, "*Do you know what my favorite verse is? Psalm 118:17: 'I shall not die, but live, and proclaim the works of the Lord!'*"

Tina sat there, stunned. Speechless.

The nurse continued, her voice strong and unwavering. "*I have a sheet of Bible verses I love to keep at my desk. I share them with people who might need to hear from God. I'll grab one for you.*"

That paper—those scriptures—became something sacred to us. We laminated it. To this day, it's still on our refrigerator.

God didn't shout from the clouds that day. He didn't remove the cancer. He didn't even stop the chemo. But He answered Tina's prayer. With a knock at the door. With a nurse who couldn't have known the weight Tina was carrying—or the words she had just prayed moments earlier.

God saw her. And He sent a message, through a stranger in scrubs, straight to her weary heart: *I am with you. You will not walk this alone.*

That day, Tina began the long road of reconnecting with God. She still had to fight. She still had to suffer. But she didn't have to wonder anymore if He was there. His steady love had broken through—right in the middle of an ordinary hospital room.

Sometimes the most profound encounters with God don't come with flashes of glory. They come with a knock. A verse. A whispered, "*You will not die, but live.*"

One evening, several weeks into her second round of chemotherapy, we received a phone call from Tina's close friend, Dawn. She would often take Tina to doctor appointments and they'd go to lunch afterward and talk for hours. Dawn loved Tina's unwavering faith and joy in the Lord, that she eagerly shared with anyone who would listen. Dawn's voice on the line was both kind and resolute.

"Have you asked the elders to anoint Tina with oil and pray for healing," she asked, *"like it says in the book of James?"*

She quoted the verses from James chapter five gently, almost like a reminder from heaven: *"Is anyone among you sick? Let him call for the elders of the church, and let them pray over him, anointing him with oil in the name of the Lord..."*

I hadn't asked. But I was deeply grateful she brought it to my attention. That simple, faithful question opened the door to something sacred; something unforgettable.

I called Pastor Dave Courtner, shared that Dawn had called, and asked about the passage in James. Our senior pastor, Dave Marks, was away on sabbatical, but Pastor Courtner discerned the spiritual urgency and broke protocol to reach out to him.

By then, word had spread throughout the congregation. People knew Tina's cancer had returned, and that it was serious. Cards began pouring in from friends and family, each one filled with words of hope, love, and inspiration. So many came that we hung four rows of string across our living room wall just to display them all. Christina, who was about seven at the time, proudly called it "the wall of faith."

The anointing was scheduled. Pastor Marks came back from his sabbatical just for that moment.

That night, Tina sat quietly in the center of the room—bald from treatment, nervous with anticipation, yet ready for whatever came next. The kids and I sat close around her, and the elders and deacons surrounded us, forming a circle.

Then they prayed. One by one, voices lifted, humble, honest, desperate for God's mercy. They asked boldly for healing, reverently for His will. And something happened.

"I will not die but live, and proclaim what the Lord has done."

I can only describe it as beyond the natural. A sacred stillness fell upon the room; not startling but distinct. Time seemed to pause. The presence and peace of God was unmistakable. Afterward, several of the deacons spoke of how powerfully God met us there.

From that night forward, Tina lived 18 more years with metastatic breast cancer. Not merely surviving—but living. Living with purpose, strength, and unwavering joy.

She became a living testimony to the words of Psalm 118:17.

Chapter Thirteen

Divine Orchestration

I stuffed the grocery list into a pocket and drove to the local Acme, a few blocks away. Not much had changed. Tina hadn't let the cancer diminish her devotion to our family and our kids, either. Despite its return, she poured herself into bustling days at home with Marcus and Christina.

We discovered a store called Zany Brainy in Marlton with shelves full of games, puzzles, stuffed animals—just about anything to spark the imagination. Grabbing the kids and trekking over to wander the aisles aimlessly was one of our favorite ways to spend time together. One summer evening it was already dark when I got home, but Tina needed to get out of the house after being with the kids all day. We were both tired, but we gathered Marcus and Christina and went anyway, choosing togetherness over giving in to exhaustion.

We explored slowly, keeping an eye on the kids and enjoying a simple night out as a young family. Almost out of nowhere, a woman appeared. She didn't seem threatening, but she looked at Christina for a long moment, long enough for Tina and me to exchange a quick glance. We were both on alert.

But then the woman shifted her gaze from Christina to us. She said in a voice that was both quiet and firm, *"This child is going to be very special. God's favor will be on her as she grows."*

Tina and I thanked her politely, then we took Marcus and Christina by the hand and moved on. The moment felt strangely unsettling. We didn't say much about it in front of the kids, but the encounter left us both feeling on edge. We cut what we'd intended to be a relaxing visit to Zany Brainy short and headed home.

Later that night, after the kids were asleep, Tina and I talked about how surprised we'd been by the incident. Neither of us knew what to make of the odd woman and her kind, but perplexing words. In the end, we agreed on one thing: Christina already felt special to us. Even at that age, there was a brightness about her that was hard to explain. She

I got back to the condo and put the groceries away, then made a ham and cheese sandwich. I grabbed a bag of chips and sat down to eat with my laptop open to check email. An ad for YouTube landed in the Google sidebar.

When Christina was in high school, her creativity landed her outside the usual cliques. She'd retreat to her bedroom for hours, making funny videos of herself writing, singing, and playing the keyboard we'd bought her when she was just ten years old. She and her best friend, Lauren Longo, would spend Saturdays watching the tapes and laughing at Christina's antics.

One Saturday Christina and Lauren were hanging out as usual, and Lauren showed Christina a video of a girl singing on YouTube.

"Check this out," Lauren said, and handed over her iPod for Christina to see. *"This girl has 30,000 followers, just singing on YouTube."*

Christina trusted Lauren, but she was essentially a shy girl making music and videos in her bedroom for herself. For fun. She wasn't trying to go public.

"Aww, I couldn't do that," Christina protested.

"Christina, you sing way better than this girl," Lauren said. *"You should put your music on YouTube."*

Christina and Lauren had been close since they met in elementary school at Bethel. Lauren saw something special in Christina, not unlike the woman all those years ago at Zany Brainy. For weeks Christina resisted posting her videos to YouTube, but Lauren kept encouraging her.

Then on a Saturday afternoon, Christina set up her video camera and recorded herself singing *Dear Friend* by Christian artist Stacy Orrico. Christina loved Stacy's voice, her range, and the vocal gymnastics of her riffs and runs. She patterned her own voice after Stacy's.

Christina sang *Don't Wanna Be Torn* by Hannah Montana and videotaped that, too. Then she posted both videos to her new YouTube channel, zeldaxlove64.

About a week later, the morning after she posted a cover of *Party in the USA*, Christina came bounding downstairs. *"Dad, look!"* she said, arm outstretched and iPod in hand for me to see. *"I got all these people sending messages through my YouTube saying they really like my singing!"*

At first, I didn't know what I was looking at, but as Christina kept scrolling down the list, I could see message after message ... lots of them asking Christina to cover more songs.

"Wow, Christina, that's really cool!" I said.

She was beaming, but then a frown flitted across her face. *"I think something's wrong with my messages, though,"* she said. *"When I try to delete them, they don't go anywhere."*

She handed me the iPod. I deleted fifty messages, and there were still fifty messages. Then I noticed something. *"Hey, Christina, these are fifty different messages,"* I said. Thousands of messages had come in overnight!

We started telling everyone about it, and Lauren said we should have a 100K views party. By the next day, there were over two hundred thousand views! The video had gone viral overnight.

During the next few months we watched Christina's popularity skyrocket on YouTube. Marcus was tracking her stats daily on Vidstats when he noticed Tiffany Alvord, another female singer ranked in the top 50 YouTubers. He looked up several of Tiffany's videos and messaged her on her channel.

Tiffany responded and shared that she and her family would be coming from California to visit another YouTuber named Kurt Schneider, who would be producing a high-quality video for Tiffany's channel. They planned to fly to Philadelphia then drive to Connecticut to record the video. Tiffany's mom and dad asked if we'd be interested in getting together.

When we talked about it, Tina was understandably leery of connecting face-to-face with people we met on the Internet. I called Tiffany's dad, and after our conversation I felt good about meeting in person. We agreed that they'd stop at our house on their way back from Tiffany's video and music recording session in Connecticut before heading to their hotel near the Philly airport.

As planned, Tiffany arrived with her mom, dad, and two brothers. We all hit it off over Tina's spread of lunch meat, potato salad, macaroni salad, deli fresh rolls, a huge fruit salad—I still smile thinking about it. Tina was definitely the "hostess with the mostest." She always made sure there was more than enough food to feed an army whenever we had guests. We ate, then Tiffany's brothers went to play video games with Marcus while her mom and dad talked with Tina and me in the living room.

Tiffany and Christina went up to Christina's room to sing and goof around on the guitar and keyboard. I can still hear them in my mind, but they actually recorded the whole night and posted the video to YouTube. They even covered *Break Your Heart* by Taio Cruz. That post has more than 3.6 million views.

While the girls were recording, Tina and I learned from Tiffany's father, whose name also happened to be Kurt, about her work with Kurt Schneider.

"Schneider is a great kid," Kurt said. *"He's studying at Yale, and he knows his stuff as far as music videos and this YouTube thing. He's seen Christina's videos and told us he wants to write a song and produce a high quality music video for her, too."*

He asked for a pen and paper to write down Kurt Schneider's contact info.

"You guys should give him a call," he said, and handed me the note.

We hung out with the Alvord family all that night. Tiffany and Christina wished they lived near each other and already felt like the best of friends. The Alvords left our house as the sun was coming up, just in time to make their flight back home to California.

Not long after that meeting we reached out to Kurt Schneider and arranged to drive up to his family's home in Connecticut for him to record Christina. He and his parents graciously lent their beautiful condo for the indoor scenes, and the outdoor filming was done in a lovely park near Yale University.

Kurt had arranged a song especially for Christina made up of lines taken from various Miley Cyrus songs. *Miley Medley* was Christina's first high-quality music video, and over the years it's garnered more than 4.3 million views. The song was such a hit that Kurt invited Christina to record a second music video with Sam Tsui for a cover of Nelly's *Just a Dream.* To date, the video has more than 238 million views on Kurt's YouTube channel and over 27 million on Christina's.

Especially as Christina's popularity on YouTube exploded, Tina made sure our kids' lives were as "normal" as possible. In the background she bravely and quietly endured what seemed like endless rounds of chemo.

One afternoon we were at the University of Pennsylvania for the usual battery of tests and follow up visits. Between appointments we were making our way toward the cafeteria to grab something to eat when we got a call from Marcus.

Tina cheered Christina on while bravely battling breast cancer

"Dad," he said. He sounded excited. *"I think Selena Gomez's manager is trying to get in touch with us."*

I laughed. Even I knew Selena Gomez was a star on the Disney Channel. *"Really? What makes you say that?"*

"We're getting messages from someone who says he's Brian Teefey, her stepdad," he said.

I paused for a second, then said, *"Well, if that's true, give him my number."*

Christina was quickly becoming internet famous, and that phone call marked a major turning point in her career.

Later the same night, we got a call from Mandy, Selena's mother. She was on location with Selena filming the movie *Monte Carlo*, but she and Brian wanted to talk about possibly managing Christina's career. She shared that several friends and colleagues had encouraged them to branch out and manage other artists, but Mandy had been hesitant.

"We're only good at this because we love Selena," she said. *"We care deeply about her—that's why we've been successful. If we were to manage someone else, it would have to be someone we truly believe in and care about."*

And then she said something that laser-focused both Tina's and my attention.

"We've fallen in love with Christina," she said. *"Not just her voice—but her heart, her spirit. We want to meet her and get to know your family. Would you be interested in meeting?"* There was genuine excitement in her voice—not just about a business opportunity, but about a potential relationship.

A few days later Brian flew into Philadelphia and drove over to our home in Marlton to talk about Christina's future and how he and Mandy could help guide it. He sat at our dining room table with a yellow legal pad and a pen. With humility and experience, he walked us through what it would look like to attempt navigating the music industry on our own versus partnering with someone who knew the terrain. He wasn't pushy. There was no flashy pitch. Brian was patient and thorough.

Tina and I had a quiet sense that God was opening a door to more than just a career. He had orchestrated a connection with people who believed in Christina, not only for her talent, but for who she was at her core.

We took a break from discussing contracts to go out for lunch in Medford.

Running into some students who knew Christina from YouTube and the Cherokee Idol high school talent show felt like the sign of something bigger unfolding.

Before we met, Brian and Mandy Teefey had been trying to reach Christina, but we'd missed them in the avalanche of comments on her YouTube channel. Then, Christina posted "*Special Thanks to: my awesome brother, Mark (dude on the bench),*" with a link to Marcus' channel. We finally connected when Marcus spotted Brian's messages.

Tina and I had committed to walking through only the doors God opened, and this felt like one of them. We didn't take it lightly. What made the decision to sign Brian and Mandy to manage Christina so peaceful was the love behind their offer. The Teefeys weren't just proposing management. They were offering a genuine relationship. And we didn't ask God merely to bless our plans; we asked Him to make us wise.

As Christina's career blossomed, Tina and Christina traveled to California often. Brian and his family welcomed them with open arms, even putting them up in a small cottage on the property of Selena Gomez's home. In the unpredictability and fierce competition of the music industry, their kindness was encouraging, and their support was foundational to Christina's success almost from the beginning of her career. In fact, Christina earned her first paycheck as an extra on the set of a commercial Selena was filming for her Kmart clothing line.

Tina, Christina, Marcus, and I watched from a huge mobile home camper set up for Selena and her family near where the commercial was being shot at the edge of an open field. As lunch was being brought in, Selena appeared, seemingly out of nowhere, with paper plates and napkins and began serving us. I will never forget the kindness and humility of Selena Gomez smiling and scooping food onto all our plates. She made us feel welcome and cared about.

Brian, Mandy, and Selena always treated us like family. Christina fondly christened Brian, *"Brian the Lion,"* because of how fiercely and lovingly he looked after what was best for her as he and Mandy managed her music career.

On our journey with Christina, this moment stands out as an unmistakable marker of divine orchestration. Tina and I weren't networking or chasing fame for Christina or Marcus. We'd been in a hospital grabbing lunch when a phone call shifted the trajectory of our lives.

Chapter Fourteen

Abiding Time

I finished lunch and got up to put the dishes in the sink. It was still awfully cold out, but I felt like taking a drive along the coastal road, the way I had with Tina and the kids so many times over the years. I got in the car and drove through Ocean City on Asbury for the trip south toward Stone Harbor.

Over the course of 2012, Tina and Christina moved to L.A., then Marcus moved there after high school to attend Musicians Institute. With another year before I could retire from Verizon, I went back to work in NJ. I stayed with my dad and our family dog, Chloe in the house where I grew up and made the trip out to California as often as I could. But living on two coasts, being separated from my family got old, fast.

It was hard to remain patient. I felt like my heart had already gone ahead of me to California, while my body had been left behind, still living thousands of miles away in New Jersey. It was a strange season, an in-between chapter that, all these years later oddly feels like the life I'm living here on earth—separated from my wife and daughter until we're reunited in Heaven.

Back then, in 2012 while we waited for God to reunite our family I had time to think about and practice waiting for Him to move without striving to make things happen on my own. God had spoken to me in the early '90s about staying connected to Him in an extraordinary way that I will always cherish. At the time I was a field technician at Verizon, driving a lift truck from job to job. The work was predictable, with long stretches alone at worksites or on the road with nothing but the hum of the engine to keep me company. I had loads of time to think. Nothing about it felt particularly spiritual. It was just work.

Our family with dog Eli in the early 90s

And yet, during that time, Scripture started surfacing in my mind. Not whole verses. Just fragments; a phrase here, a few words there would float up in my thoughts while I drove to work, or while I was up in the bucket doing repairs. They felt familiar, like echoes from somewhere deep inside my subconscious, but I couldn't remember when I'd last read them or heard them taught. There were no references—no book, chapter, or verse. Just words that lingered. I had the distinct feeling of wondering where these thoughts were coming from.

Then one day the phrase arrived clearly and settled in my mind: *"The truth will set you free."* I knew Jesus had said those words, but I didn't know where. When I got home that night, I pulled out my Strong's Concordance and searched until I found them in the book of John:

"If you abide in my word, you are truly my disciples, and you will know the truth, and the truth will set you free."

One word caught my eye and wouldn't let go: *abide.* I looked it up and found it meant "to remain, to stay, to continue." My NIV Bible translated it as "remain." The simplicity of it struck me. Faith wasn't striving, or proving, or achieving. It was staying connected.

After that, the verses kept coming. Sometimes I had to pull my truck over just to find a scrap of paper and write down a phrase before it slipped away. At first, I thought it was coincidence; random thoughts surfacing from things I had read or heard at church on Sunday. But after days of it happening, I began to recognize a pattern. The verses circled around the idea of connection again and again: the vine and the branches, remaining in Christ, the grafting in of the Gentiles, God's mercy and grace—a relationship connection, not just performing acts or doing things.

Within a week or so I had so many scraps of paper that I decided to start writing them in a notebook. When I showed Tina my handwritten notes, she offered to type them up for me on her typewriter at work—it was long before laptops. When she finished, there were four typewritten pages of verses gathered from those quiet moments on the road.

At the time, it didn't feel dramatic. There was no defining event attached to it. No big decision. Just ordinary days filled with small reminders. Tina was fighting for her life, battling cancer with almost every ounce of strength she had. Marcus and Christina were still little, still needing snacks and baths and bedtime and comfort. I was working to provide for our family and be strong, trying to come home each day ready to help Tina and love our children. My parents were stepping into the gap to help us any way they could. And in the midst of all of that, God was teaching me to abide. The work was quiet, almost hidden, but it was shaping me for seasons I could not yet imagine. I was learning to trust that the same God who speaks in the crisis also speaks in the quiet.

By the time Marcus and Christina were in their teens, Tina and I were keen to lean on God, watching and listening for when He was drawing people into relationship with Him, or directing us to make a change in our own lives. As she became more popular on YouTube, and Brian and Mandy became her managers, Christina was confident she needed to be in Los Angeles to make the most of opportunities to write, sing, and collaborate on music.

In 2010, Tina and Christina were traveling back and forth for weeks at a time between Philly and L.A. What had first seemed temporary was starting to feel like a pattern–like the Bible verses teaching me to abide. Patterns have always had a way of getting my attention.

I was initially focused on the practical; I saw what it was costing us every time the girls made the trip–plane tickets, hotel rooms, rental cars, meals–it was becoming endlessly expensive to live between two places. But underneath the dollars and cents, the circumstances themselves seemed to be nudging us. It was as though life was quietly insisting that we consider this to be more than a series of trips.

Tina felt it, too, from her own vantage point. She saw how beautiful California was, and a place that was once unfamiliar was beginning to feel strangely comfortable. She also knew it would be much easier not to live in constant motion. Ditching the packing and unpacking, flying back and forth, adjusting and readjusting–she relished the thought.

One evening as she and Christina were walking from their rental car to their hotel, Tina asked a simple question. *"Christina, do you miss New Jersey?"*

Christina answered with the kind of honesty that comes from youth's lack of a filter. *"No, not really. Is that wrong?"* She added, *"I miss Dad, and Marcus, and my own bedroom...but no, not New Jersey."*

Loving life in L.A.

I had begun sharing my thoughts with a couple of trusted friends, telling them that circumstances were beginning to dictate a possible move to California and asking them to pray. After much prayer and conversation, both men suggested I bring up the idea to Tina.

Tina texted that she wanted to talk, and I replied that I'd been wanting to talk to her, too. The ensuing phone call felt almost scripted.

"I've been wanting to talk to you about something," I said.

"I've been wanting to talk to you about something, too," Tina replied.

"Well, you go first," I said.

"No, you go first," Tina said, before finally spitting it out. *"I think we should move to California."*

I laughed softly when she'd said the words, not because it was funny, but because it was so clear. *"That's exactly what I was going to say."*

That moment meant more to me than the decision to move, itself. Tina and I had separately arrived at the same conclusion. Neither of us had talked the other into it or planted the thought in the other's mind. Somehow, while carrying different pieces of the same burden, we'd been led to the same conviction. Over the years, Tina and I would often see God work that way in our lives–not through spectacle, but through convergence. Through prayer, through circumstances, through quiet agreement, we developed a growing sense that the path before us was being made clear one step at a time.

We talked more when she and Christina got back home, then decided to tell the kids what we were thinking and hear what was on their hearts about it. We called Marcus and Christina into our bedroom.

"Your mom and I have been talking about moving to California, and we want to know what you both think." Then I asked them a question that had been stirring in me for some time. *"Do you think something bigger than just us is going on with Christina's popularity on YouTube?"*

Marcus answered immediately, with the kind of clarity that came from what seemed obvious to him. *"Yeah, Dad. I don't think Christina is manipulating the numbers on YouTube."*

There was something in that moment that felt weightier than a family's decision to relocate. It felt like recognition. Not certainty about every detail, not a guarantee that every step ahead would be easy, but a shared awareness that something was unfolding that was beyond our own planning or doing. We were not creating it. We were responding to it.

"Yes," Christina quickly chimed in. *"Mom and I were talking about that in California. It would be so great!"*

That the girls would move first became pretty clear. We found an apartment, then Marcus and I loaded up a twenty-six foot Penske moving truck, hooked up the family car behind it and headed west. Tina and Christina would fly out a week later. That trip is one of my favorite memories with my son. We took turns driving, laughed often, and shared that mixture of exhaustion, excitement, and wonder that comes whenever life begins changing for real.

In just three days, we crossed the country and arrived early Saturday morning on January 28, 2012. We unloaded everything into the apartment, returned the rental truck, then found a place to eat nearby. The Pro Bowl happened to be on the tv, so we ate and watched. I still remember the odd simplicity of that moment. After exerting all the effort, driving all the miles, and feeling all the emotion of moving our family across the country, there we were just sitting in a restaurant, eating a meal, and watching football on a Sunday afternoon. Life-changing moments are not always draped in grandeur. Sometimes they're wrapped in paper napkins, tired silence, and the peace of giving in to rest.

On Monday, Marcus and I picked up Tina and Christina from LAX and brought them to the apartment. For a brief moment, with the four of us there together, it felt as though the future had arrived—but we would need to patiently rely on God to get us *all* living in California. We moved the girls in January, then Marcus in August after graduation. We were trusting God that at the right time, it would be my turn. I kept saying that it would be obvious. We just needed to abide in Him and pay attention.

Then Tina and I had that fateful meeting with Mike Frost and T Santora in Burbank setting the plan in motion for me to retire from Verizon in New Jersey on March 30th and be rehired at AT&T in California on April 1st. We were all full of hope that I would soon join my family there permanently. At that point, it was mid-January and I still had a few months before I could retire, so a couple days after that meeting I flew back to New Jersey.

The very next day, literally the day after I got back from California, I was working on site near the hospital in Burlington off of Route 38. Around three o'clock my phone rang. It was Tina.

"I think I broke my leg," she said.

"What?" I knew I'd heard her right, but I couldn't believe it.

"I think I broke my leg," she said again, and the words came pouring out of her. *"Christina and I were walking through the foyer of our apartment on the way to IHOP to get breakfast, and I just collapsed. I was laying in front of one of the doors to another apartment, and the woman heard the commotion and came out and called the ambulance and told us which hospital to go to. We're at Providence Hospital. They think I broke my leg."*

She paused to take a breath.

I was still trying to let what she said sink in.

"I'm so sorry," Tina said. *"What now?"*

"It's okay," I said. *"Let's just wait until we hear more from the doctor, and we'll figure it out."*

Little did I know, I was on speaker and Christina could hear what I was saying. She grabbed Tina's phone.

"Dad!" she said, *"You gotta come back right now! Get on a plane and get out here as soon as you can!"* She sounded near breathless with conviction. *"Mom's leg is broken. Don't wait for a doctor. Get on a plane, and get out here now!"*

I smiled, remembering the many times we laughed about that call over the years. Tina and I were the adults, but Christina's teenage panic pointed us to a blessing in disguise: God's hand at work through Tina's broken leg. I felt like He'd paved the way for me to use my vacation and sick time to make the move happen quicker.

I thought back to those verses about abiding from my days on the road. They'd resurfaced time and time again. God was teaching me early that spiritual life isn't built on isolated moments of inspiration. It's formed by daily choosing to remain, to stay connected when nothing spectacular is happening, or when your plans seem to be interrupted by the pain and inconvenience of a broken leg.

Through joy, through success, through grief that tested everything I believed, that truth held fast. The life of faith wasn't about chasing extraordinary experiences. It was about abiding—remaining when life made no sense. Staying connected when the road turned dark. That relationship with God was the thread that held everything else together.

I wondered if God must have thought we were dense. With all our going to Bible study and listening for His voice, paying attention and watching for His hand moving in our lives, we almost didn't see that the next leg of our family's journey with Him would be in California.

God had spoken to me then, teaching me what it looked like to trust Him in the good and bad times. He spoke to me now in 2018, through every memory as I visited the places that so powerfully connected me to my past. His still, small voice whispered of His steady love. I'd come home to New Jersey desperate to reconnect with God, to find Him again for myself, and He'd met me here. With every memory He'd reminded me of truths He'd revealed as I'd lived the past forty years of my life.

I threaded my way south and eventually onto the Garden State Parkway, wanting to revisit the town where I'd grown up. Outside my parents' old house on Franklin Avenue I felt filled with peace. Once sleepy, small town Berlin now bustled with activity and traffic all around me. Walmart Superstore and Marshalls bookended the quiet neighborhood of my childhood. People milled about buying groceries at ShopRite and DIY supplies at Home Depot. The field where us kids used to play whiffle-ball or hide-and-seek in the tall weeds was now smooth black asphalt teeming with cars and shopping carts. McDonalds and Taco Bell beckoned, less than a five-minute walk from where I sat—which would have seemed like a dream come true to me as a teenage boy.

This place and everywhere I'd been in the past two weeks had been my first home. It was where my life began, where I'd grown up, met my wife, seen my children born. I had found faith in God for myself here.

As was my habit, I arrived at the airport a couple of hours before my return flight to Los Angeles. My mind filled with thoughts of what lay ahead. Now with Tina gone, Marcus and I would carry on the work of the Foundation. We'd push forward to honor Christina's and Tina's memory.

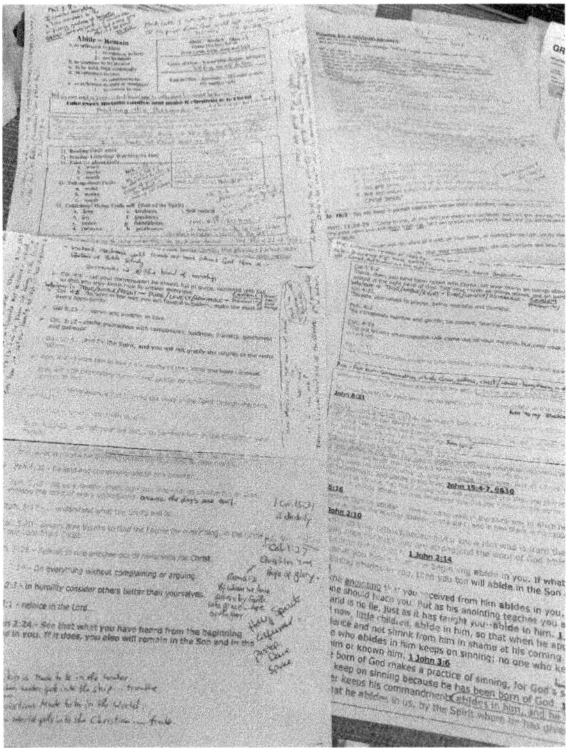

Tina typed up my scrawled notes on abiding

As the plane carried me west toward California, I sat quietly by the window, letting the low drone of the engines steady my thoughts. I realized that something in me had shifted.

Behind me were two weeks of solitude in Ocean City and memories of my family and our life before Christina's career took off. Ahead of me was the life I was returning to, with all its now familiar roads, responsibilities and griefs still waiting for me. The ache had not disappeared. My questions had not all been answered. But something in me had settled. In the quiet of those days beside the ocean, on the boardwalk, praying in conversation with God and reliving memories my heart had been drawn upward again, realigned vertically, back toward Him. And now, just like all those years ago when I'd trusted Him to move my family across the country, it was time for me to trust God to return me to the home Tina and I had made in California.

Chapter Fifteen

Christina's Rise to Fame ... and Glory

I thought about our family's decision to move to L.A. now as I made my way back there after my time alone in Ocean City. Marcus and our dog Chloe awaited me, but I knew Tina's absence would feel like all the life had been sucked out of the home we'd shared together for so long. I determinedly shifted my thoughts to happier times.

Tina and Christina were the first to move in 2012, but once the whole family was relocated life seemed to overflow with California sunshine and the endless excitement of seeing Christina's music career blossom. The weather and beauty of the place was even good for Tina as she lived through cancer treatments. We were together, and despite the cancer, nothing felt better than that.

Christina's love for music began long before the whirlwind of YouTube and adoring fans that catapulted her into the spotlight. When she was little, Tina sang to her all the time, especially at bedtime. Christina sang before she talked, began playing the piano at four, and wrote her first song at seven years old. Tina made sure our home was a place of love, where our kids felt accepted and cherished. She was an only child, and she didn't want Marcus and Christina to experience that kind of loneliness. She often joked that she came from a broken home and married into a "*Leave It To Beaver*" family. Then she joyfully created her own.

Left: Christina Victoria Grimmie

Bud, Marcus, Christina, and Tina

I loved hearing Christina talk about how close we were as a family and how much that meant to her. Each of us had our own special relationship with her. For Christina, Tina *was* the party, someone she could always count on for fun. Marcus was her cheerleader and best friend. And she and I could always talk candidly about our faith. We loved Christina just for who she was.

When she was seven, Tina and I gave her a karaoke machine, and from then on she'd spend hours in her room singing along with the music to her favorite songs. We bought her a keyboard when she was ten, and she added piano playing to her singing in earnest. Christina could play all of her favorite songs, and later practically any song, by ear.

When Christina was little we asked Jacqui, a friend from church, to give her piano lessons at our house. Ten minutes into her first lesson, Jacqui called us into the room with the piano. She looked at us and said, *"Watch this,"* then to Christina, *"Do you know the song from The Little Mermaid?"* Christina nodded and began playing it. Jacqui said, *"I think you need a different type of piano teacher for her."*

And once, my sister Carole spent months learning to play *My Heart Will Go On* by Celine Dion. After she finished, and while we were all congratulating her, Christina sat down beside Carole at the piano and effortlessly started playing it.

Christina plays with Aunt Carole

The world might never have believed it watching Christina's videos on YouTube or seeing her perform, or listening to her in interviews, but before she took the spotlight, Christina thought of herself as just a shy girl from New Jersey who loved to sing, make music, and play video games in her room. She first sang publicly at church, but ran off stage when she missed a lyric. She was something of a hidden talent to everyone–even to us, at first.

Then, one day Christina came home from classes at Cherokee High School and casually remarked to Tina, *"I signed up to sing in a contest at school."*

Tina's eyes widened. She was about to speak, but Christina went on. *"It's called Cherokee Idol ... kind of like American Idol, and the audience gets to vote."*

Tina just stared at her in disbelief. *"Christina,"* she said, *"you won't even sing in front of us, and now you're going to sing in front of an audience at school?"*

It was hard to imagine. At home, Christina could be in her room singing her heart out, but the moment my hand touched the doorknob, the music stopped cold. She was that shy about letting us hear her. So when Tina told me what she'd done I could hardly believe it myself.

But when the night finally came, there we were, walking into the Cherokee High School Performing Arts Center. The place seated around fifteen hundred people, and it was packed.

I can still feel the energy in that room, the anticipation, the crowd. And then our Christina stepped onto that stage. She sang *"Halo"* by Beyoncé, and for those few minutes, the girl who kept her voice to herself stood in front of a full auditorium and let it soar.

Christina finished second that night, but she was so happy just to have done it. The next day at school a lot of students were saying she should have won and floating theories about why she hadn't. But Christina didn't care about any of that. She was quick to say how talented the winner was and that she deserved to win. That was Christina–she never seemed interested in promoting herself above someone else. She let her talent speak for her.

Not long after Cherokee Idol, Christina sang in a battle of the bands competition at another high school. A talented musician in his own right, Marcus helped pull a group together to back her and joined them on lead guitar. That time, they won first place. Little by little from then on, the gift Christina had hidden behind a closed bedroom door was finding its way into the open.

Marcus and Christina win high school Battle of the Bands

Christina was also teaching herself how to record on GarageBand. It was simple software, but for her it became a doorway for expressing her creativity. She used it to begin shaping her own songs and recording her own ideas. Before long, we were sending several of her originals off to be copyrighted.

Looking back now, those moments feel so precious. At the time, they seemed like small beginnings. But they were really the first glimpses of what was already there, a gift quietly growing, waiting for its time to be heard.

It felt good to be back in our family home in California. I climbed the stairs and thought about how shy Christina had been in those early days. It took a lot to coax Christina out of her shell, but when she took the stage, people found it hard to believe that such a powerful voice could come out of such a little girl. Her Sunday school music teacher once asked Tina and me, *"Do you know what you have here?"*

Before she posted her first video to YouTube, Christina's music was private, something just for her. It was as though God had given her a treasure that was hers alone for the first fifteen years of her life. Then, in 2009, it seemed she was ready, even eager, to pursue her dreams. She never set out to be famous or make lots of money—she just wanted to get her music out there and be a role model who inspired people to be the best version of themselves they could be.

Christina found confidence and the courage to be herself in her relationship with Jesus, and she wanted everyone to experience being loved by God the way she knew she was. She was steadfast in that, but she never tried to force anyone to believe what she did. She never shied away from talking about her love for the Lord. Sometimes she'd send someone to me with questions–with a smile and an enthusiastic nod, she'd say, *"You need to talk to my dad!"* After that, she often said she left it up to God to do the rest. Her responsibility was to show her faith by the way she lived.

When Christina started gaining popularity around our small hometown some people at church wanted to know why she sang secular songs instead of Christian music. I'll never forget how clearly and confidently she answered:

"There are many female singers in the Christian music industry ... Amy Grant, Jaci Velasquez, Twila Paris, etc., but are there any young female singers who are Christians singing pop music? And talking about their faith in God?"

Tina and I believed God loves us for who we are, and He wants every aspect of our lives to reflect our relationship with Him—but that won't look exactly the same for any two of us. Christina modeled that belief to perfection.

I like to think God used some of my experience to inspire Christina to stand for Him. In the summer of 2001 when I was at Verizon, I was partnered with a guy named Wayne Lewin. During lunch breaks we'd eat and talk about work, and eventually our conversations ventured into life and faith. We discovered we had going to church, serving in ministry and studying the Scriptures in common. We began meeting an hour before work in my car on Monday mornings to pray for our families, for the men we worked alongside, and for the entire Verizon garage. It wasn't anything formal. We were just two guys showing up early, asking God to work in a place that felt more about schedules and machinery than spiritual things. Within a couple of weeks other men at work asked to join us. That turned into a men's Bible study and prayer group that got too big for meeting in a parked car. We asked for and graciously received permission to meet in an unused office inside the Verizon building.

On Monday, September 10, 2001, about ten guys showed up. The next Monday, September 17, nearly fifty men crammed into the tiny room. Between those two Mondays, 911 changed the world. People were searching for stability, for answers, for something solid to stand on.

Often guys would ask, *"Bud, your prayer and Bible teaching is so helpful. Why aren't you a pastor?"* I'd answer quickly: *"You and I would not be having this conversation if I were a pastor in a church."* I knew God wanted me to help people get to know Him wherever I was. In the midst of 9/11 His pulpit was my job as a splicer for Verizon, leading Bible study in an empty warehouse office. God turned co-workers praying in their cars into a safe haven in a world that didn't care about Him until it was turned upside down.

Christina dared to be herself in the world and encouraged others to do the same. A self-described video game nerd and *"the biggest Zelda geek in the world,"* she live-streamed from her Twitch while playing as *zeldaxlove64*. She even created her own version of the Triforce—a sacred relic in *The Legend of Zelda* made of three pieces representing power, wisdom, and courage. For her, the pieces were food, music, and video games, all united under Jesus, the true embodiment of Power, Wisdom, and Courage. Christina showed Christ's love by being herself and sharing Him in every aspect of her life.

The Elvish Princess by Christina's friend, Cassie Wills

Zeldaxlove64

Christina and I had many conversations about faith and the Bible. We talked often about standing for Jesus in an industry that didn't care about honoring Him. Christina was determined to remain true to herself, true to her belief in God despite the pressure to conform that came with fame and fortune.

When asked about what she would do with the platform she had gained while competing on *The Voice* in 2014, Christina's answer summed up her commitment to representing Him well, no matter what. *"Jesus Christ is the reason I can even sing. It's not my voice, it's His. And I will use it, win or lose, for His glory."*

Christina refused to be someone she was not. I once asked her to listen to a song called *Held* by Natalie Grant. She listened and enjoyed it. We talked about how much the song meant to her mom and me spiritually.

"I get the concept, Dad, but I don't have real life experience with it, personally, like you and mom do," she said.

I asked if she'd consider recording the song for her YouTube channel. And in her beautiful, transparent honesty, she graciously said she didn't think many of her fans would understand the song or why she chose it.

Now that she's gone, I wish I had asked her to record the song just for me.

Christina understood the people God sent her to serve. In just six years, she came to know and love her fans deeply and sincerely. To her, they were more than fans; they were friends and fans, or *"frands"* as she affectionately christened them. She so appreciated them for supporting and encouraging her, no matter what, despite what she saw as her flaws, their love was steadfast. She wrote the song, *"With Love"* to describe their undying and unconditional love for her. During a concert in the Philippines she sang the words with tears streaming down her cheeks–because everyone in the audience was singing along. They knew every word.

Later, I shared with her how the words of the song impacted me. *"Christina, your lyrics express the way God loves us."*

The realization brought amazement and joy to her eyes. She always marveled at how God seemed to speak love through her singing and songwriting.

Untold numbers of people all over the world found the courage to be themselves and love themselves despite anyone else's opinion because of Christina's example. She shared her insecurities—being self-conscious of her nose flaring when she sang, and being called "horse" by a kid in school, or knocking over a water bottle and obsessing over it during a live performance—and she shared that mess ups didn't define her. Christina was a beautiful girl, but she didn't care about being pretty. She wanted to reach people struggling to see their own inner beauty.

"Be yourself, and have a good time! Be stupid, be dumb, be funny; be who you are," she'd say, sometimes while crossing her eyes, sticking her tongue out, and twisting her features into an impossibly goofy expression. Her fans found her relatable and sincere, and they loved her for being that way.

It still amazes me how much Christina accomplished in just six years in the public eye. She garnered millions of subscribers and views on YouTube—to date her videos have nearly a billion views. She impressed music superstars Adam Levine, Usher, Blake Shelton, and Shakira, turning all four chairs on *The Voice* Season 6 blind auditions.

Christina The Voice Season 6

She dominated the iTunes charts just behind Adele. She twice toured internationally as the opening act for Selena Gomez. She won countless awards and accolades, including the first-ever *American Music New Media Award* celebrating her massive online presence—at just seventeen.

Christina lent her time and talent to causes she loved and won awards for helping raise money for PETA, the Humane Society, UNICEF, and breast cancer research and awareness.

Christina took the world by storm and accomplished all that she did without a long-term endorsement from a mainstream record label—instead she credited her success to God and the love and support of her adoring fans.

Confidence is not, "They will like me." Confidence is, "I'll be fine if they don't."

And yet, in success or disappointment, Christina grew as an artist, but never changed as a person. She shared her love for Jesus openly and stayed true to her values. She loved her family wholeheartedly and remained the warm, funny, encouraging person she'd always been. Christina never stopped getting emotional over her frands' heartfelt comments on her YouTube channel. She loved to shout out to them: *"Team Grimmie, you RAWWWK!"* She opened her heart and arms to them without reservation.

Christina and frands

***

I walked down the hall to my office, the room that had once been Christina's music room and sat down. I put my elbows on the desk and let my head drop into my hands. Sometimes you see the hurt coming for someone you love and you know it's necessary; you know it's for the best, even though you wish with all your heart you could stop it.

The thought reminded me of when Christina was about six months old and due for her next baby vaccine. Tina came down hard with the flu the day before. We could've rescheduled. Any reasonable person might have. But I looked at Tina, pale, aching, barely able to sit up, and something in me rose to help her. *I've got this,* it said. *"I'll skip work and take Christina for her vaccination."* I said it boldly, the way a man sometimes does when he's trying to convince himself as much as anyone else.

I knew the routine, having taken the kids to the pediatrician a few times with Tina. So I packed the diaper bag, buckled Christina into her car seat, and drove to the doctor's office, still feeling that strange mixture of fatherly confidence and quiet uncertainty. Christina was in one of those bright moods that make you feel like the world is safe. She babbled and smiled and waved at strangers like she'd never known disappointment.

The waiting room wasn't crowded. It was calm in a way you don't usually get in a doctor's office full of sick people. Christina sat on my lap, behaving so well. She was so happy and pleasant, almost angelic. She looked up at me and smiled. A thought crept in and landed on me with a little weight: *If she knew why we were here, she wouldn't be smiling like this.*

And then the questions darted around in my mind the way they do when you've got too much time and not enough control. *Is this going to really hurt her? Is it just a quick prick and we're back in the car and heading home? Will she even notice?*

Our name was called, and we walked down the hallway to a small room. We sat. We waited. Christina kept smiling like she trusted the whole world.

Then Dr. David walked in. I'll never forget the shift in Christina's demeanor. She saw the doctor and something inside her changed instantly. Her little body stiffened. Her eyes grew wide. She crawled up and clung to me as though she'd suddenly realized this wasn't a playdate. This was something else.

She wasn't being logical—she was only six months old. Her response was pure instinct. It was that built-in alarm God put in us somewhere deep, long before we can put words to anything. But my adult mind had no trouble voicing her unspoken questions.

Dad, who is this? Why does this feel wrong? Where's Mom? What's happening?

And I did what fathers do. I looked her in the eyes. I spoke softly and made my face calm. I pulled her close and settled her down. I even got a little smile out of her as she relaxed on my lap, trusting me again, trusting that my arms meant safety. But I knew I couldn't always keep Christina safe, snuggled and protected in my lap. And maybe instinctively, I had the thought that not every battle is physical.

In a flash Dr. David moved in with the syringe and expertly jabbed Christina's pudgy little arm. It was over before she knew it, all but the delayed tears and screams. Christina forgot that moment, but I never did.

Yes, sometimes you see the hurt coming and realize the pain is ultimately for good. And sometimes you don't.

***

As usual, the morning of June 10, 2016, I woke up before my alarm. I noticed a text from my friend JD that had come in late the night before. Christina had been talking about moving closer to the studios in Hollywood, and he'd found a house that she might like in the Woodland Hills area.

I decided to take the PCH in to work on what started out like just another beautiful day in Southern California.

Later in the day I got a call about data lines being down for several businesses in the Playa Delray area. I met a coworker there and as we were troubleshooting the problem, we both realized it was going to be a long night. It was Friday, and I had requested an "on time" quit. I hoped it would be honored, but after hours in the hot sun with no breeze, we still hadn't gotten the lines back up. It was getting close to 5 o'clock, so I called Tina to let her know I probably would be late getting home. I was still hoping my supervisor would find someone to replace me for the night.

The kids were preparing for the concert in Orlando. They wanted to head to the airport immediately after to catch a red eye to LAX. Their next show was just two days away at the Troubadour in LA, a legendary, intimate live music venue in West Hollywood, California. It was famous for launching the careers of Elton John, The Eagles, Guns N' Roses, and countless other artists and songwriters. Her producer Stephen Rezza had arranged for her set to be a showcase for talent scouts from the A&R departments of three different record labels.

"Could we bring Marcus's car to Jonathan's that night so it would be there when they arrived on the red eye?" Tina asked. *"Marcus wants to bring Christina home right away to get some rest and start preparing for the show. It could be a big deal for her career."*

Even though the kids' big plans sounded exciting, I was exhausted after the long day I'd had.

"You'll have to follow me to Jonathan's to bring me home after I drop off Marcus' car," I said. We left it that I'd call Marcus to discuss the details.

I drove along the PCH toward home. It was not yet dark, but the sun was going down. I dialed Marcus's number. I still remember the stillness, waiting in the quiet to begin a phone call that would change my life forever.

Marcus answered his phone, his breathing extraordinarily heavy.

"Dad, Christina was shot."

"Shot?" I couldn't grasp what he was saying. *"She'll be OK right?"*

"I don't think so, Dad," he said. *"I don't think so."*

"Well, she has to be, Mark..."

I don't remember any conversation after that. We hung up, and I tried to decide whether or not to call Tina. I thought it would be much better if I were with her when I told her. I decided it would be much worse if she heard what happened as breaking news or from someone else who'd heard it as breaking news. I called my wife.

I can still hear the sound of Tina wailing.

"Call everyone we know that prays," I said. *"Ask them to pray for her to survive."*

By the time I got home, I felt relatively confident that God would allow Christina to survive. I had convinced myself that her injury was not that bad.

When I got home Tina wanted me to call Marcus. We stood in the kitchen as he answered. He was no longer breathing heavily; his voice just sounded eerily calm, like someone in shock.

"How is Christina?" I forced the words out.

"Dad, Christina is gone," he said. *"She's gone, Dad. She's gone."*

He told me he'd grabbed the shooter's arm, and they'd spun around, falling to the floor and jarring the gun loose. The man had stood up first and pulled another gun, and suddenly it was like he was pushed up against the wall. He then shot himself.

I've relived that conversation so many times over the years. I still cannot imagine what my son went through that night. My heart breaks for him and what he witnessed.

Brian and Mandy Teefey were at our house in a flash. Friends Maurice and Robin LaMarche also got there quickly, along with their son Jonathan and his best friend, Jonathan O'Rourke. Tina and I were paralyzed with grief, our minds unable to comprehend what had happened.

Maurice and Robin purchased our tickets, and the two Jonathans escorted me to the airport. Tina was too emotionally devastated to travel. The Teefeys and the LaMarches stayed with her. At the airport, O'Rourke kept several steps ahead of us, deftly parting a way for us through the crowds and explaining the situation to the attendants at the airline counter. Jonathan LaMarche never left my side. I will be forever in debt to those two young men for stepping in to care for me that night.

I was out of my mind. I remember so very vividly repeating, *"Everything looks so different. Why has everything changed?"* The lights, the people, the signs—suddenly everything looked vastly different.

We arrived in Orlando, and the two Jonathans settled me into the hotel where we were staying. The next morning I opened my eyes and just as I was awakening, I felt an incredible relief that it was all just a dream. Then the realization slammed back into me—it was not a dream. My pain was unbearable.

I somehow got up and dressed. I made my way to the lobby, where I was surprised to find my friend, Joe Longo, Lauren's dad waiting. He'd been in a conference in Orlando and heard the news that morning. He'd found out where I was staying and rushed over.

Christina had been touring with the pop/rock band, *Before You Exit.* Joe drove us to the house of band members Connor, Riley, and Toby McDonough.

Their mom, Joan McDonough shared the moments she and her sister had spent with Christina just before she went off to the meet and greet table.

"My sister wanted to meet Christina," she said, *"so we went backstage after the show. We prayed with her, and my sister said, 'God is good!'"*

Christina cheerfully answered, *"All the time,"* and hurried off to meet fans and sign autographs.

My sister, Carole, and my nephew, Nicky met us at the McDonough's. Their pastor came, and someone began reading lines from one of Christina's favorite songs, *In Christ Alone.* Overnight, Christina's cover of the song went viral, with nearly 4 million views.

Later, at the sheriff's department, we met with detectives assigned to the shooting. It was early in the investigation, but they shared the details of their findings to that point. Afterward, Michael Moresche, the lead detective, escorted us back to the airport. Through tears, Marcus and I talked quietly about trying to hold on to God, even now. I will always remember what the detective said to us on the ride over.

"Unfortunately, I have seen a lot of this," he said. *"But I want you to know that you're going to be OK. I've seen families fall apart after a tragedy like this. Depression, divorce, substance abuse, and even suicide rates skyrocket,"* he said. *"But I can tell you you're going to be OK, because I've been listening to what you've been saying."*

We never know how our reaction to tragedy might be impacting someone else's view of God.

"You have displayed a strong faith in God," Detective Moresche said. *"Hold on to that."*

Getting back home to CA is still a blur. I don't remember much of anything. Just Tina. Tears and dark sadness. We unpacked in painful silence, trying to settle back into a house that no longer felt the same.

Somewhere in the middle of it, the grief that had been pressing against my chest broke loose. I began to sob, crying out to God with the only words I had.

Why, dear God, why? Why Christina?

I sobbed until my voice was barely a raspy croak. The anguish poured out of me, reaching a crescendo in one desperate thought:

What could possibly be worse than this?

Suddenly, unmistakably, an answer came. Not audibly, but with a clarity so sharp and distinct it stopped me in my tracks as though the words had been spoken straight into my soul.

If she hadn't known Me.

Instantly, I stopped crying. The gnawing ache didn't disappear, but something in it shifted. A wave of gratitude rushed in so suddenly, so powerfully, that even now I struggle to explain it. Christina did know God. She had not merely heard about Him from a distance. She belonged to Him. She trusted Jesus in a real and personal way. And that realization changed everything.

I grabbed my phone and called Tom Horner. When he answered, I could barely contain what I needed to say.

"Thank you for not giving up on me all those years ago, Tom," I said, my voice choked with emotion.

When I had mocked him, laughed things off, and pushed back against the truth he was sharing, he kept praying. He remained faithful to God's command to share the Gospel. And now, I could see with overwhelming clarity that had I never come to faith in Jesus, Christina might never have believed, either. And that, I knew with utter certainty, would have been far worse. Unspeakably worse.

That realization was something I could cling to. The pain was still there. The loss was still crushing. But that sudden piercing moment of awareness that as heartbreaking as it was that Christina had died, it would have been irreparably worse had she died without knowing God. The revelation was so far beyond my natural way of thinking, I knew it had come from Him.

And the thought made me ask the question all over again with fresh urgency and deeper seriousness: *Is the Bible true? Can I trust the Scriptures?*

I could hear Tom Horner asking, the year before I joined the Navy: *Do you know where you'll go when you die?*

Did I truly believe that Jesus was publicly crucified, and that His death paid the price of admission to Heaven? Do I believe He then presented Himself alive, proving the debt was paid?

Because if He is alive, then the promise of resurrection is not poetry, not sentimental or wishful thinking offered to grieving hearts. It is reality. It is something solid enough to stand on when trauma, pain, and death seem determined to pull everything down around us. That hope, set against the darkness of losing my daughter, was exactly what I needed in order to keep going. I would not give up on living.

I had hope. Not a new kind of hope, but the same hope that first stirred in me back in 1977, when my journey to a right and deeper relationship with God began. Now, I had hope that I would see Christina again; hope that Tina and I could somehow survive the devastation that had entered our lives. Hope that I would not give up on Tina, or on Marcus. I had hope that love, even wounded love, still had something to hold on to.

I remembered the little Bible tract Tom had given me years before. It offered evidence that persuaded me that Christianity was not built on fantasy, but on truth that could bear the weight of scrutiny. And with renewed determination, I began digging deeper again, not merely into arguments and evidence, but into my relationship with God.

Chapter Sixteen

The Shoreline of Heaven

Of course, Marcus was Christina's hero. She adored him, not just because he was her big brother, but because Marcus is the honest, loyal, and steadfast person everyone wishes they had standing by their side, no matter what. From the moment Christina came into our lives, Marcus took his responsibility as her big brother to heart. He was always there to cheer her on and to encourage her to be herself. He was always there to tell her, *"You be you."*

When he was little, Marcus loved anything to do with building or construction. I remember him watching for hours as an excavator dug and moved and piled dirt on a lot across from where we stayed one summer on our family vacation. It didn't matter to Marcus that we were just steps from the boardwalk, and beyond lay the sandy beach and sparkling ocean. His face lit up at the sight of a dump truck or a bulldozer, even a rider mower, so a trip to the local hardware store with "Pop"—my dad—was a dream come true for him. But even that paled in comparison to spending time with his baby sister.

Once, when Pop wanted to take him to Home Depot, Marcus asked, *"Is Christina going?"*

"No," Dad said.

"I don't wanna go then," Marcus answered without a second thought.

Christina was shy when they were growing up, and she cried when she couldn't go with Marcus on his first day of kindergarten.

Albert Sr. and toddler Marcus

Tina and I built a close-knit family to nurture the kids' relationship when they were little, but even as young adults they remained best friends. And their friendship is something we treasured. Christina often introduced Marcus to her fans from the concert stage while he played guitar behind her. She loved to shout, *"Everybody say hi to my brother, Mark!"*

Marcus and Christina supported each other in everything. At Bethel Church, long before the spotlight found them, they ran out and hugged at center court during a Salao soccer match after a tough play. The other players' parents couldn't believe it. *"We can't get our kids to hug at home in the kitchen, let alone in front of a crowd of their friends!"*

When Marcus and Christina were in high school, Fellowship Alliance Church launched an outreach program called *Teen Alpha* to help students explore questions of life, faith, and God. The concept was disarmingly simple: invite people to a meal, offer a twenty-minute talk on life and faith, then sit around tables and discuss. No pulpit pressure. No raised hands. Just food, conversation, and honest questions.

Tina and I were eager to support it since Marcus and Christina were teenagers at the time, so the four of us attended the initial interest meeting. We watched a short Alpha promotional video that cast a compelling vision of honest conversations, spiritual discovery, and lives changed by encountering Jesus. After the video, our youth pastor, Mike, stood up.

"Would you be interested in helping start the program here at the church?" he asked the group of parents and students. Tina and I raised our hands. We were in. A few other parents also volunteered. That's when Marcus pulled me aside.

"Dad," he said, *"if adults are leading the table discussions, the teens aren't going to open up. They'll say what they think the adults want them to say, but not share their honest feelings and opinions. You need to let students lead the groups."*

I paused for a moment, realizing he'd made a valid point. *"Go tell Mike,"* I said.

Straightaway, Marcus walked over to him. I watched as he shared his thoughts in front of Mike and several others. To his credit, Mike didn't just brush him off. He looked Marcus in the eye and said, *"That's a great point. Do you want to be one of the leaders?"*

Christina and Marcus in concert

"Sure," Marcus replied.

One by one, other students stepped forward, volunteering to lead as well. The parents organized food, prepared materials, and set up the weekly sessions, but the teens led the conversations.

And something powerful happened. The discussions were lively and raw. There were questions about God, Jesus, prayer, doubt, and temptation. Teens wrestled openly with what it meant to follow Christ in high school. Questions weren't filtered for approval. Faith came up against real obstacles: peer pressure, parties, identity, and loneliness. There were debates and laughter. It wasn't easy, but it was honest. There were moments that felt sacred, as though God was leaning in to listen.

Marcus and Christina, best friends

But after the Alpha program ended, there was no real follow-up. No next steps. Everyone drifted back into their routines. And by the end of the school year, Marcus noticed something that troubled him. Many of the same students who in January had led and taken part in Alpha, students who once talked passionately about following Jesus, were drifting. Many fully immersed themselves in behavior they lamented during Alpha–partying, drinking, drugs, and sexual promiscuity. Old habits resurfaced and flourished into the summer. The excitement for godly living faded, and with it, so had the commitments.

Marcus saw what was happening and came to a hard, honest conclusion: *"It feels manipulative,"* he said. *"Who's going to say no to a free pass to Heaven? It's easy to raise your hand and say you believe in God's grace just to stay out of hell. But if there's no change, no follow-through, what does it even mean?"*

Marcus and friends at Teen Alpha

Marcus wasn't being cynical. He wasn't rejecting faith—he was questioning the version of faith that counts raised hands and emotional responses but forgets discipleship, accountability, and transformation.

"It's just easy believe-ism," he said. *"Say the prayer. Count the numbers. Celebrate the converts. But nothing really changes."*

Marcus stepped up because he believed authenticity mattered. Appearances didn't impress him. He wanted substance and a faith that could stand up in real life and win against temptation, peer pressure and the quiet drift of compromise.

Those conversations with Marcus have stayed with me. Rather than judging, he was yearning for something deeper—something real. In the tension between what is celebrated publicly and what is lived privately his young mind began forging a conviction: faith must be more than a decision. It must become a way of life, or it's not worth following. Over the years I've learned that minus a deep and abiding connection with him, *it's not even possible.*

In a world full of emotional highs and quick spiritual fixes, what does it mean to truly walk in *steady love* with God? How does one grow roots and endure—not just for a moment, but over a lifetime? Marcus' questions echoed in my heart, too, punctuated by another, forged in the face of unimaginable pain and loss: *How do I trust God when He allows evil to strike down the innocent?*

My prayers from the time Christina was young would often end with, *"Lord, keep her safe, and well, and pure."* Yet God had allowed her to be murdered. The God I believed in and prayed to and worshiped in church on Sunday mornings had not kept my daughter safe and well.

So, the anger I directed at myself I eventually turned toward God. I was Christina's father. I should've listened to Tina always asking about more security, but I bore the burden of failing to protect our daughter. I remember knowing, not just thinking or feeling, but knowing it was my fault that Christina was dead. I was supposed to protect her.

But another idea insinuated itself into my thoughts. *God was our Father; had He not also failed to protect her?*

Some Sunday mornings I'd try to go back to church for comfort and answers. I'd make it partway through the service, and the words of a song would cause me to walk out. There were darker things working on my mind, trying to tell me who God was.

He is not a "good, good father."

God had allowed my daughter to be taken from this world–*to where?* I knew Christina still existed; she had not been annihilated, but *where was she now?* I could not let go of the question, yet posing it brought me unexpected comfort.

There was something healing in asking it–not because it removed the finality of death, but because it drew my heart toward the promises of God and away from the emptiness of despair.

In some ways, missing Christina reminded me of the seasons when her career had taken her to far away places like Germany, the Philippines, and Singapore. We missed her back then, too. She was on the other side of the world, gone from our sight. She was living in places we could not see, experiencing things we could only imagine.

When she was around nineteen years old, Christina went back to New Jersey for an event at a local mall. She was staying with my dad and visiting friends while she was there. She called one afternoon to let us know how things were going. She and Tina chatted, and Tina filled me in as the conversation went along. At some point, Christina says she's going to New York to attend a video game convention.

"Oh," Tina said, *"well, who are you going with?"*

"I'm going with a friend I met online," Christina answered. She sounded so excited. She was already on the NJ Turnpike, headed to New York.

"Tina," I said, *"gimme the phone."*

Tina handed me the phone. *"Christina, turn around at the next exit,"* I said. *"Don't go to New York by yourself."*

"Dad, I'm a big girl," she said. *"I travel all over. I can take care of myself."*

By that time Christina had already been on an international tour with Selena Gomez.

"Christina, don't go to New York by yourself to meet someone you've only ever met online," I said.

That made her angry. *"But my friends are all waiting for me,"* Christina said. *"I'll feel like a fool if I don't go! Like some little girl whose parents won't let her go!"*

"That's right," I said. *"Your friends will have it right."*

After more back and forth we agreed to a compromise. When she got to the parking garage she'd call and stay on the phone with Tina and me until she met up with her friends.

"I'm here," she said when she called. *"I found a good parking spot in the garage, and I'm walking up to the convention center, about to go inside."*

She walked through the doors and said, *"Oh, there's my friend and his friend–"*

And then there was nothing. The call dropped. I kept calling her number and getting no response.

Tina and I were thinking the worst–we completely took the "panic now, ask questions later" route.

I called my sister Carole, who had taken Christina to and from the mall event.

"She said she was going to New York with Sarah and Lauren," Carole said.

"No, she went by herself," I said. Tina and I found out that Sarah's parents wouldn't let her go. *"We were talking to her one minute, then the next, she just disappeared. I keep calling and texting, but there's been no response for over half an hour."*

Carole was mortified. She was ready to get in her car and drive to New York when I got a text from Christina.

Christina: *Hi, Dad. Sorry we got cut off.*

Me: *What happened?*

Christina: *Bad service in the bldg?*

Me: *How do I even know this is really you? Anybody could have your phone and be texting. Call me.*

When she called, I could hardly contain my anger.

"Christina, your mom and I are having a heart attack," I said. *"Aunt Carole's about to drive to New York–"*

"I'm sorry, I didn't know," Christina said in that way teenagers have of implying that their parents are overreacting.

When Christina got back home to California things remained cool between us. We interacted politely, but the tension was palpable. I was still angry, and she was still defiant.

"I didn't like what you did, Christina," I said. *"I didn't agree with that."*

"Dad, it was fine," she said. *"Everything was okay. It was no big deal."*

Things went on like that for a few days with us barely speaking, until one night, Christina came downstairs to where Tina and I were sitting in the living room. Her eyes were filled with tears.

"Dad," she blurted, *"I am so sorry."* She had just watched an episode of a crime show about a girl who'd been alone and victimized in New York. She had googled more info about young girls falling prey to crime in New York. It terrified her.

She was heartbroken over the thought of her mom and me worrying, not being able to reach her.

We hugged and talked, forgave each other and promised to do better in the future.

Christina and Marcus would both continue traveling the world. Tina and I learned to endure our kids being away a lot of the time. Of course, the separation of death is not the same. The distance between life and death is unfathomable. But without Christ, it would feel like complete and permanent loss. Gone. Lost, forever.

But because Jesus lives, that was not the story I was left with. Christina was not lost. She was with him. I recalled the Bible verse that said for the believer, to be absent from the body is to be present with the Lord. She was in God's presence. How could my daughter be physically dead, but spiritually alive? What does it mean to be in God's presence, in Heaven? *What is it like where Christina is now?*

The question wracked my mind, gnawing at my thoughts. I reached out to men who knew me, who knew Christina, and who knew God deeply and asked them to pray for me because I was near drowning in the overwhelming loss.

Pastor Dave Marks, a dear friend and spiritual mentor recommended I read *Heaven*, a book by Randy Alcorn. In nearly 500 pages, Alcorn does a deep dive into everything the Scriptures say about Heaven and reveals it to be so much more than the vague, ethereal–and honestly, for me, boring–place of eternal clouds and harps of my childhood Sunday school memory.

As I read and began searching the Scriptures about Heaven more intentionally, I thought about the first believers, those who watched Jesus die and saw Him alive again. How Heaven filled their thoughts, shaped their relationships and directed the way they lived each day. To them, Heaven wasn't distant or theoretical. It was real. They believed Jesus when He said He was making all things new. They embraced Heaven as an undefiled place–pure and good, with music richer than any we've ever heard, and art that reflects beauty without distortion. They believed there would be trees, skies, oceans, and animals, all untouched by decay. Relationships would be characterized by unconditional love, free from pride, jealousy, greed, and bitterness. Love would flow unhindered. Life would be punctuated by joyful discovery, meaningful work, and even friendly competition.

They imagined connection as God meant it to be–and their imagination couldn't contain even half of it. But I had never gotten that kind of clarity in church.

As Christians, I believe we've lost sight of what's ahead and what our future truly holds. The idea makes me think of Florence Chadwick, the first woman to swim the English Channel in both directions and a renowned world-record holder. She once set out to swim from Catalina Island to the California coast, but while she swam a dense fog settled around her, and after nearly sixteen grueling hours in the cold water she began to falter and had to be pulled out. Later, reflecting on that moment, she said, *"If I could've seen the shore, I would've made it."* When she tried again just two months later, the fog was just as thick, but this time she succeeded because she kept a mental picture of the shoreline fixed in her mind the whole time she was swimming.

Despite the fact that Tina, Marcus, and I were reeling from the loss of Christina, God didn't halt the relentless progress of Tina's cancer. It remained a dense, blinding fog in our lives. But in turning my thoughts heavenward, something started to come into focus: the same God who once looked over His creation and called it *"very good,"* and who walked with man in the garden in unhindered fellowship has not abandoned that design. What was lost in Eden, He has always intended to restore. The story doesn't end with separation and brokenness. For believers in Christ, it moves toward joyful reunion with our loved ones and our God, who is nearer than our next breath.

***

I remember my last morning with Tina as clearly as though it happened yesterday. We had traveled to Mexico on the advice of a trusted friend to try an alternative course of cancer therapy. Tina's hospital room had become our temporary refuge during what would be her final round of treatment. Another hospital bed had been placed right next to hers, so I could stay by her side. I had woken up twice during the night, stirred by the sound of Tina's heavy, labored breathing. Each time, I walked back to the nurse's station and asked if they could give her something to help her rest.

Both times, the nurses responded with more medication. Both times, Tina drifted back to sleep. The third time I woke up was around 8 a.m. Her breathing was worse—louder, harder, more urgent. I got up quickly and went to the nurses' station again. Then I came right back to Tina.

I stood on her left side, leaned over, pressed my cheek to hers, and whispered, *"I'm right here, Teen. I love you. The nurse is coming to help you sleep."*

Then, out loud and with all the desperation of a husband fearing the loss of the love of his life, I prayed: *"Lord, please show up in this room. Right now. I need You to show up."*

In my mind, I was thinking something dramatic—a bright light, a thunderclap, a sign I couldn't miss. Something. *Anything.*

And then I thought, *Where is that nurse?* I was starting to feel frustrated, even angry. *Why were they taking so long?*

Suddenly, Tina's breathing quieted. Her labored gasps gave way to stillness.

I looked into her face, startled. Amazed.

The Lord answered. Not with a thunderclap, but with peace.

And then I noticed—Tina wasn't breathing at all.

I gently lifted her right eyelid. And in that moment, I knew. She was gone. She had passed from my arms into His. A strange, supernatural peace began to wash over me.

Just then, the nurses entered the room. I stepped aside and quietly said, *"She's not breathing now."*

They moved to confirm what I already knew. Tina had passed from this life to the next.

As I stood near her bed, I began to hear something. At first, I thought I was imagining it; maybe it was in my head. But the sound grew slowly, steadily. It was singing. A choir. Soft and faint, a melody rising in the back of my mind; the words repeating over and over: *"I hear the cry of every longing heart... worthy is the Lamb."*

The words were so clear, and yet I didn't recognize the song. The music kept repeating—those same words, over and over, like a refrain caught in my spirit. I hadn't been listening to music recently, not in the hospital, not in those long nights. And yet here it was, unmistakable.

I sat down on the bed beside Tina's still body. I reached for my phone and typed: *"I hear the cry of every longing heart..."* and Google finished with, *"worthy is the Lamb."*

And there it was. *"I Will Rise"* by Chris Tomlin. I read the lyrics in stunned silence.

I found the song on YouTube and listened. And as I did, I wept. It was like God had personally placed that song in my heart before I even knew what it was. He had personally answered my desperate prayer. *"Show up in this room,"* I cried, and he'd done it. Not in thunder. Not in a flash of light. But in the quiet ushering of His daughter home.

That morning in Mexico, God reminded me that He doesn't always show up the way we expect. But He always shows up.

He knew what I was about to face. He knew I would be living the rest of my life without Tina; I was already living without Christina. He knew how much the weight of loss would cost me. Gratitude came before understanding, as in that moment, He did what only He could do. He gave me *peace.* He gave me *presence.* And He gave me a song I didn't know I needed.

"I hear the voice of many angels sing... worthy is the Lamb."

I will never forget that moment. I thank the Lord for catching Tina. For catching me and holding us both when I had nothing left. Glory was no longer an abstract promise to me. It had become the only horizon big enough to swallow up sorrow like this. I needed God more than ever. In that, I'm not unique. I believe that each of us longs deeply to feel connected in a loving relationship with God.

All those years ago at Teen Alpha, and the night he found the courage to step between his beloved sister Christina and unspeakable evil, I believe Marcus tapped into something about our longing, our need for a relationship with God: *We are not meant to get through the trials of this life without Him.* God can help us soar in a moment of inspiration, or desperation, but He also wants to walk with us through the valleys when the emotion wears off. Abiding faith in God isn't just a spark—it's a flame that must endure and grow, because none of us gets through this life unscathed.

***

November of 2018 marked just over two months since my Boo—my Tina—went home to be with the Lord. This morning, like every morning since September 2nd, I missed her. There was no more cancer. No more being poked and prodded. No more labs, tests, procedures, or endless doctor appointments. And for all of that—I was thankful. But I missed the thousands of small, sacred things that made up our life together—the conversations, the laughter, the routines, even the disagreements. I missed her presence in the house, her voice, her eyes, and the way we moved through life, side by side.

I think of Jesus and how He called His disciples not just to believe, but to *follow*—to walk with him, to learn from him, and to be changed by him over time.

It was the kind of faith Christina had. Faith that made her seem to love God with a wisdom beyond her years. The night she was killed I received a text from an unknown number as I boarded a flight to Orlando. It was a quote of Christina's: *"Sometimes God allows terrible things to happen in your life and you don't know why. That doesn't mean you should stop trusting Him."*

It was the kind of faith that made Tina choose being better rather than bitter, despite the cancer. That's the kind of faith Marcus was hungry for. And it's the kind of faith I want to keep growing in myself—the kind of faith that's built on an abiding relationship with Jesus.

God's steady love isn't afraid of the long haul. It shows up when the church lights dim and the music fades. It keeps going when no one's counting conversions or taking photos for the newsletter. Steady love stays when the concert ends and the crowd scatters. It shows up in the words of a song that reminds us of how intimately God walks with us, sometimes carrying us through the thick fog of this life toward the destination He's had in mind all along. Like Florence Chadwick, I was learning to keep my eyes focused on the shoreline of Heaven.

Christina and Tina were now in the presence of God, in Heaven. As I studied, I began to see that Heaven is not some distant place, some vague existence, but the fulfillment of a promise God has been making from the beginning. Both Testaments of Scripture speak of a new heaven and a new earth, a restored creation where God will dwell with mankind again in a world devoid of pain, death, suffering and sorrow, forever. What we feel now, the groaning, the longing, the sense that this world is not quite as it should be is not meaningless. God has placed that longing in us as a kind of guarantee, a reminder that something greater is coming; that what is mortal will one day give way to eternal life.

Over the years, that realization has changed something in me. If you can't see the shore it's easy to lose heart. But catching even a glimpse of where you're headed can give you the strength to keep going. For me, the shore of Heaven is no longer just an idea or a vague concept. It's a promise. It's being with Jesus in a restored world where God walks with His people and wipes away every tear. And I believe this: the clearer that shore becomes in our hearts and minds, the more courage we have to endure, the more joy we carry, and the more urgency we feel to share that hope with others. I'm sometimes weary. Sometimes the weight of enduring this life feels like too much, like more than I can do. Having a relationship with Jesus is like seeing the shoreline of Heaven–and He gives me the strength to go on.

That's not to say I've abandoned all thoughts of joy in this life. On the contrary, I believe the things we love here that are pure and good, like heartfelt joy and laughter will not be lost, but fulfilled. I've often said I married Tina because she laughed at my jokes. And I remember when she and I stumbled upon an episode of *Seinfeld*–we were practically rolling on the floor. I could always make Christina laugh, too, even when she didn't want to. And Marcus and I are hardcore fans of *Airplane* and the *Naked Gun* movies–he's sent me memes about them that still crack me up. As broken as this world is, marked by tragedy, suffering, and the many sorrows that weigh on us, we still find ourselves loving it–because there is real beauty here. Those things aren't Heaven, but they're glimpses of it.

Tina and I had just returned to California after Christina's funeral and memorial service in New Jersey. We were physically exhausted and emotionally drained–our hearts heavy with a grief that words couldn't touch. After unpacking and settling into the stillness of our home we decided to sit in the hot tub that afternoon, just the two of us. Not to talk through the pain, not to solve anything or think about what to do next. Just to be together, to breathe, to rest. To find some small space to feel the weight of it all without collapsing under it.

The warm water swirled around us, and silence enveloped our backyard. It felt like sacred space, as though God had pulled back the curtain between Heaven and our backyard and flooded it with comfort, with peace.

We had never noticed any hummingbirds in our backyard in the years we'd lived in our house. But that day, as Tina and I sat in shared sorrow, a rather large hummingbird suddenly appeared. It hovered about three feet in the air and faced us; directly, unmoving. We turned to look at each other, surprised. Then we looked back at the bird. Then back at each other.

"Look how bright it is," Tina whispered. The hummingbird shimmered with the most vibrant green–Christina's favorite color. We sat transfixed, caught in the moment long enough to see the bird clearly, long enough to feel the weight and wonder of it. And then, it was gone.

I don't believe Christina was that hummingbird. But I do believe that God, in His infinite compassion and aching love for our broken hearts, caused that moment to happen, a holy interruption. The Creator, who commands all things, even to the smallest of birds reminded us that He sees. He is in control. And that Christina, our precious daughter, is under His care.

That moment didn't take away the pain, but it gently whispered a truth we needed to hear. God's love doesn't always come with answers, but we can trust His promise of a new heaven and a new earth, where everything that has broken our hearts in this life–cancer, violence, loss, death–will be gone. Not covered over, but eradicated, completely and finally. Jesus came to earth, lived on earth, walked its roads, and touched its people. He will one day return to earth. He will not abandon His creation, but restore it. Renew it. Redeem it.

I often think that if we really want to get even just an inkling of what the new earth will be like we shouldn't just look up, we should also look around. In September after Christina's passing, Tina, Marcus and I attended the wedding of very dear friends. Matt and his parents, Bruce and Hope were more like family. Marcus, Matt, Adam, and Austin, nicknamed the Rat Pack, had been friends since kindergarten, and Marcus was Matt's best man for the wedding. Under a beautiful blue Texas sky, crisp white chairs dotted an emerald green lawn. Family and friends gathered joyfully around a fairytale gazebo to witness and celebrate the wedding of Matt and Kaylyn.

A reminder of God's steady love

Tina and I found our seats as somewhere behind us guests marveled at a beautiful, huge monarch butterfly fluttering overhead. Even as the crowd grew, one seat remained empty next to Tina. We turned to look at the butterfly, and it fluttered in our direction. When it reached us, it flew around Tina and me before alighting on the vacant seat next to her. We fully expected it to flutter away at the slightest movement, but instead it sat, majestic and beautiful, unfazed as Tina got out her phone and took pictures of it.

Again, I am not one to think that the butterfly was Christina. But I do know that God is sovereign over all things. I believe that He loves us and wants us to trust Him through even the most difficult times...through the worst of times as well as through the good times. He reminds us that He's got us, and that He's near. And He promises to one day reunite us in His presence with those He's taken to Heaven before us.

Chapter Seventeen

Coast to Coast and Back

God had been blessing and comforting me with His presence in the years since 2018 when Tina passed and I returned to California after spending two weeks reconnecting with Him in Ocean City. I felt Christina and Tina were near too. I believed that in Heaven with Him they were more alive than they'd ever been. I knew in my heart that my girls were okay and that they were right where they were supposed to be—even as I prayed for God to carry me through the pain of living in this world without them. I was committed to being the best man that I could be for God, despite my loss.

God had also been putting on my heart the idea that I should be near my dad during this time of his life. My dear friend, Tony Scott, who had given me the 100-day goal journal after Tina died, had himself died in 2022. While I worked through the journal, and even after that, I grew more convinced that I should be with my dad in the last years of his life. But I also felt torn about leaving the fellowship of godly, faithful men who had become like brothers to me in California; men like Tony, whose friendships were hard to come by.

I'd felt a similar need for men's fellowship back in December of 2017, when the loss of Christina was still an open wound.

Left: Marcus and Summer on their wedding day

My girls are okay and right where they're supposed to be

Tina and I had been attending Reality L.A. and loved the people there, but Tina was feeling less and less able to go out. The drive felt long, especially when she stayed home. When I went alone, I left part of me with her. Reality Carpinteria was closer, and the drive was nicer, but Tina only went a few times. The problem remained–if she didn't go it felt like too much time away. And most Sundays she just wasn't up to it. After a few weeks I ended up not going at all.

I started looking for a church closer to home and found Calvary Westlake. After watching a few videos on their website I decided to go one Sunday. There happened to be a guest speaker that morning, a missionary who delivered a fine enough message, but nothing in it seemed to land with me. The music was incredible, but seemed almost too polished. I felt like I was watching the worship rather than entering into it. The place just felt too big, too impersonal. I left feeling more unsure than when I'd arrived. On the short drive home I wondered if maybe I should simply stay home on Sundays. I could read the Bible and listen to sermons on my own. This was before COVID, before online church became a thing, but the thought was there.

Later on at home I found myself back on Calvary's website, scrolling without much expectation when a thought crossed my mind. *I wonder what the men's ministry is like?*

Over the years I had come to understand that a church's men's ministry could be a good indicator of its spiritual health. Women's ministries seemed to grow and thrive organically, but when men showed up hungry for God, it usually meant there was something spiritually real for them there, too. Calvary's men's ministry met on Saturday mornings at seven o'clock. Initially I thought that was pretty early, but being an early riser, it dawned on me that the timing was perfect. The church was close enough for me to go and be back by eight-thirty or nine, when Tina would probably just be getting up.

The next Saturday morning I took the ten-minute drive to Calvary, pulled into the church parking lot, and was immediately dismayed. The lot was huge, but there were only two cars in it. Two. I sat there for a minute looking out over all that empty pavement, wondering if I'd come too early or misread the time. I got out of the car anyway and walked to the entrance and through the open doors. Inside, signs pointed the way to the men's ministry in Room 2104. Still unsure, I followed them upstairs and into a room full of round tables set up with chairs—and just two men sitting together at one of them.

"Good morning, I'm Jay," one of the men said. Smiling, he stood up and introduced me to the other man, whose name was James.

I explained that I lived nearby and was looking into the church. After we exchanged a few pleasantries, I finally asked what I had been wondering from the moment I pulled into the parking lot.

"Am I early? Is this all that show up?"

Jay smiled. *"It's the Saturday before Christmas,"* he said. *"We're off this week, but James and I come anyway, in case someone shows up."* Then, he added, *"Like you."* He went on to tell me that there were usually around fifty men there on a normal Saturday morning.

I was immediately humbled. What I had mistaken for weakness was actually faithfulness. What I had judged and found lacking turned out to be a generous loving kindness from the Lord. Had I walked into a room full of fifty strangers that morning, I probably would have kept my story tucked inside me. I would have smiled, shaken hands, and stayed near the edges. But instead, God gave me just two men. Two men who loved Him and obeyed when He said, *"Show up for the ones I will send you."*

I joined Jay and James at the table, and before long I began sharing what had weighed so heavily on my heart. I told them about Christina, how I had lost my daughter to gun violence and how I was wrestling with God over it. I told them about Tina and her more than twenty-year battle with breast cancer. I shared enough for them to understand that I was not simply church-hopping. I was desperate to find some place, some fellowship, some solid ground to stand on while life was constantly giving way beneath me.

They listened with such kindness. They did not rush me. They didn't offer shallow answers. They simply heard me. Then they prayed for me in a way that truly lifted my soul. They assured me that after the holidays I would meet more men who loved God, loved His Word, and were committed to helping each other honor Him with their whole lives.

Looking back, I see God's hand at work in all of it. Instead of being lost in a crowd at Calvary Westlake, He'd sent two brothers in Christ to meet me, personally. I have attended ever since, and God gave me more than a church there. He gave me brothers, friends, and fellow disciples. Later, when COVID pushed so much of life onto screens, He kept us connected through our Bible study on Zoom, where I met another true laborer in the Lord, Jack Mellin. And later still, I began facilitating GriefShare and met Kay, Jeff, and Jan.

Grief doesn't shrink over time; life grows bigger around it

During that time I stumbled across the Tonkin grief model—that grief is like a ball in a jar, filling the space until there was room for nothing else–but that in time though my grief remained, the jar of my life would expand to hold new relationships and experiences; my life would grow around my grief. And when I was strong enough, through the grace and unfailing love of God, I began to share the idea with others as part of a genuine pathway to hope.

Over the years during Saturday morning men's study at Calvary Westlake, God prompted me to put into words a simple morning prayer that I could return to each day. I had been inspired by my dear friend Matt Dalton, who shared in our men's group how much of God's word he'd been able to memorize simply by reciting it in prayer each morning. My own prayer would also remind me of how God had drawn me closer through the triumphs and tragedies–and even the mundanities of my life. After Tina passed away, I had found community and ministry in California, but I was unsure how that would fit with this longing to be with my dad in New Jersey. And what would become of the desire God had placed on my heart for discipling and mentoring men?

In California I was also enjoying having two puppies in the house. Our family dog, Chloe, had died in 2021, and it had been a year before we adopted Indy and Navi. The time and effort it took to raise and train them was a welcome addition to my life. If I was moving back to New Jersey to be near my dad, I wanted to bring the dogs with me. And I didn't want to just stick Marcus with the responsibility of looking after them. He also had a life of his own: he planned to marry his fiancé, Summer, in July.

Marcus and I were returning home to California after a Christina Grimmie Foundation event in March of 2020 when the country shut down due to COVID. I became a hermit of sorts, reading the Bible, journaling, meditating, and reflecting on who God is and what I believed He wanted from me. In the quiet of the pandemic, God's voice seemed to speak louder about moving closer to my dad.

I flew out three or four times during the year to visit him, my sister Carole, and other family members, but the feeling of wanting to be near Dad more permanently persisted. For eight years Carole had driven nearly an hour from her home in Somers Point to visit Dad in the assisted living facility where he lived. Each week she checked his medications and made sure he had groceries. Every trip back to New Jersey confirmed in my spirit that I should be spending more time with my dad and helping my sister look after him.

Marcus and Summer

So, I began to look for places to rent for a possible move. Apartment hunting from across the country was difficult enough, but COVID restrictions and needing a place that accepted dogs made the search feel almost impossible.

In May of 2023, friend and former Evesham Township Mayor Randy Brown asked Marcus to come to New Jersey to work with his daughter, Ryan, on a live music set. Ryan was a huge fan of Christina's, and Randy had hosted a town-wide vigil in Christina's honor after her death. I decided to tag along to spend a week with Dad and to visit with Carole and family.

Marcus and I boarded the plane and settled in for the five hour flight. We talked off and on about the upcoming changes in our lives. He and Summer were getting married. I was planning to take the dogs and move back to New Jersey to be near my dad. At some point in the conversation, Marcus mentioned that me moving with the dogs wasn't the only option.

"Now that Indy and Navi are older and trained well enough, Summer and I can look after them," Marcus said. *"You don't have to take them with you."*

I'd always planned to take the dogs with me, but if I ended up leaving them Marcus and Summer could still spend a year or so with the house to themselves as newlyweds.

"That would be a game changer," I said, suddenly more optimistic about the possibility of finding an apartment in New Jersey to be close to Dad.

We landed on Friday night, and Marcus was to meet Randy Brown the next morning for breakfast. He invited me to come along. We got to the restaurant and spotted Randy sitting in a back corner booth with his mom, Eileen Brown, whom we'd met previously.

"Hi guys," Eileen said as we approached the table. *"I hope you don't mind. Randy told me you were coming to have breakfast, and I just wanted to see you again. I live in the apartments across the parking lot, so I walked over."*

"Of course," I said. *"It's great to see you!"*

She and Marcus exchanged greetings, and we all sat down.

"It's funny you mention apartments," I said. *"I'm hoping to move back to New Jersey to be near my father."*

Randy chimed in, *"Well, after breakfast we can walk over, and I'll introduce you to the office staff. I know everyone over there. You could even see my mom's place to get an idea of what the apartments look like."*

"Oh, yes," Eileen said. *"They really are beautiful apartments."*

So we walked across the parking lot after breakfast, and Randy made the introductions. Eileen graciously gave us a tour of her lovely apartment, and moving back to New Jersey to be near my dad had gone from possible to probable, overnight.

When I spoke to my sister, Carole about moving back and potentially having an apartment already lined up, she was overjoyed. Dad's rent at the assisted-living facility where he had lived for the past eight years was increasing again and would soon be more than $4,000 per month. It would take all of Dad's monthly income to cover the cost. And there were growing concerns over pending management changes. Carole and I thought that if Dad and I could rent apartments near each other, we could make it work.

Suddenly, it dawned on me—*why not rent a two-bedroom apartment and become roommates with Dad?*

I mentioned the idea to Randy, and true to his word, he kindly helped us find a two-bedroom apartment in the same complex as his mom.

What an amazing blessing living with my dad was for those eighteen months. From the first night in our little apartment in New Jersey he never stopped thanking me for taking care of him.

"What are you gonna do without me?" he'd joke. *"You spend all your time taking care of me!"*

When I moved back to New Jersey to help care for Dad I thought I was entering a season of duty. And I was. Love, I was learning, is proven most in what it lays down. But even while I was caring for Dad, God was steadily pulling me into a deeper relationship with Him. Looking back, I can see that God was not only providing for my father in his final years. He was also reminding me of how lovingly He provides for our needs, and then invites us to share His love with others.

In many ways, that season represented more than one of caring for my dad. I didn't realize how much of my own life God would have me revisit during that time. There is something about slowing down near the end of life that makes you look more carefully at how you've spent it. I was stepping into a season of remembrance, a season of taking time to notice the ways God had led me all along.

After losing my wife and daughter I developed a preference for being alone, even while living with Dad, surrounded by family and friends near where I'd grown up. And sometimes it just hurt too much to relive my losses with every new person I met. But, I needed fellowship. I needed to be around other believers, men who loved the Lord and loved His Word. As I spent time alone with God, He gently moved me to reach out and interact with other people. Solitude had been necessary, but I knew I was not meant to be alone.

By 2024 I had gone through the *Experiencing God* study many times; once with Tina after getting the book from my friend Bill, and then together with others in our home. In January I was meeting on Saturday mornings with a group of men at my friend Jeff Bennett's house. These men had become like brothers, and we spent twelve weeks walking through *Experiencing God* and memorizing Bible verses together. Out of those meetings God would bring more men who wanted to know Him better, men who were like I had been at Calvary Westlake, seeking to be discipled and mentored.

By late February, the group at Jeff's had been meeting for about seven weeks and had reached the chapter entitled, "*The Crisis of Belief.*" We were charged to add Hebrews 11:6 to the verses we'd memorized.

"*Without faith it is impossible to please God ...*"

The lesson was full of stories about churches and individuals sensing God leading them in one direction or another, moving forward in faith, and then watching Him meet needs in ways they could not have foreseen or orchestrated themselves. Hearing those stories brought me face to face with something I'd been wrestling with regarding the Christina Grimmie Foundation.

Since its inception, we'd held live events that required enormous amounts of time, energy, planning, and money. They always increased awareness. They often brought our team closer together. People were encouraged and moved by them. But financially, they rarely produced much. The community stuff was real, but the dollars did not always arrive in amounts we hoped would sustain the work. As I prayed and thought about moving forward in 2024, I began to sense the Lord impressing upon me not to hold a live event that year. There was no audible voice, just the conviction that came from the way I had learned to hear God speak: through His Word, through the counsel of other believers abiding in His Word, through prayer, and through circumstances.

Those four channels had become familiar to me over the years working through the *Experiencing God* study. And in January of 2024, they all seemed to be pointing in the same direction. The Word reminded me to trust, not strive. Prayer kept pressing the same burden on my heart. Wise believers listened, prayed, and confirmed that the thought of foregoing a live event that year was worth taking seriously. And the circumstances themselves seemed to say, *"Stop striving so hard to manufacture what God wants to provide."*

So, there in the margin of my workbook I wrote a prayer that now feels like a small altar, built in pencil. I asked God to convince me about the 2024 CGF budget. I wrote that I believed we were supposed to trust Him to provide through recurring donations alone, without a live fundraising event that year. I asked if perhaps I should instead focus on writing His story in my life and watch for Him to work out the fundraising needs. I wrote an instruction:

"Let us earnestly pray for God to provide for CGF."

The words looked good in the margin of my workbook, but at the time, the prayer felt like faith stretched thin. Looking back, I see they were faith being taught to stand. Months later, God answered in ways I could never have imagined or scripted.

In April, I received an email from *Celebrity Family Feud.* A celebrity contestant had chosen the Christina Grimmie Foundation to receive the donation of their winnings. Board member and friend Sue Procko confirmed that it was real, so I submitted the paperwork, but didn't give it a second thought.

Then in mid-June, Jeff and I were at his house talking through some controversial topics in Scripture, comparing thoughts, convictions, and questions. Somewhere in the middle of that conversation, my phone began buzzing over and over again. Finally, I stopped and checked my texts.

The first was from my sister, Carole. *"Bud, Dave was watching Celebrity Family Feud, and some young lady won $25,000 for the Christina Grimmie Foundation!"*

Then, a screenshot from my friend Phil Morgan via his sister in another state: *Tori Kelly had won $25,000 for the Christina Grimmie Foundation.*

The rush of joy I felt is difficult to describe. It was not the thrill of receiving money as though it were mine to keep. It was the thrill of knowing what it meant. It meant help. It meant relief for someone; hope delivered in a practical form.

Early September brought another moment that I'll never forget. Marcus had been touring with The Living Tombstone band for several months, and on one particular night, they were playing a venue in Orlando, near where Christina was killed in 2016. The same city. The same airport. The same streets. The same air. Marcus had talked with Summer and me about the anxiety he felt returning there. He did not quite know how to process it or what to say when people asked him about it. And truthfully, neither did I.

That night I sat in my bedroom with the tv on and the volume turned low. I tried to read, though I hardly took in a word. My eyes kept drifting to the clock. Eight o'clock. Nine o'clock. Nine-thirty. I knew the show would be over. The crowd would be mixing around. Those were the very minutes when, years earlier, everything had changed for us forever. I felt the old dread moving again, crawling under my skin.

I called my friend Tim and asked him to pray. Then I called my friend Jeff and asked him, too. My prayer was not elaborate, just simple and trembling: *Lord, please let this be a positive experience for Marcus. Please be with my son tonight. Please let there be something redemptive here.*

At 10:15 the phone rang. It was Marcus. I answered, relieved just to see his name on the screen. *"Hi Mark."*

"Hi Dad," he said, almost brightly. *"Do you know what happened?"*

The moment those words left his mouth, my heart shot into my throat. For a split second, I was back on another night, another call, another breathless voice telling me the unthinkable. I tried to steady myself.

"What do you mean?" I asked.

"Dad, the show was ending, and Sam Haft took the microphone and got everybody's attention," Marcus said. He went on to tell me that TLT was donating one hundred percent of the ticket sales from the night's show to the Christina Grimmie Foundation.

"This is for you, Christina," Sam had said, and then, pointing to Marcus, *"and for that guy right there."*

Twenty thousand dollars. Out of nowhere. I can still feel what came over me in that moment. Gratitude. Relief. Awe. A sense that God, in His tender and often surprising way, had reached into a place of old horror and planted something living there. Not as an erasure; nothing can erase what happened. Instead, He reminded me that evil does not get the final word. Not in Orlando. Not in our story. Not in His.

Then, early in December I was reviewing the *Experiencing God* lesson, preparing to share with Chris Corvo. Chris had heard about the group that met at Jeff Bennett's house at the beginning of the year and reached out to me about going through *Experiencing God*. Each Monday morning for six weeks we had met for coffee at Harvest Coffee Café to discuss what we'd read the previous week.

Marcus Grimmie, musician and tour manager for The Living Tombstone

I opened the workbook and noticed the prayer I'd written in the margin back in February:

"Let us earnestly pray for God to provide for CGF."

Suddenly it all came together. This was the very week, the very unit, *"The Crisis of Belief"* that I'd been working through back in February when I was struggling with the idea of not holding a CGF live fundraiser for the year. I had written the prayer as a commitment to trust God to provide for our budget. I realized that what I had written in the margin months before had taken on flesh in the real world. When I thought about all that happened since then, how God had indeed met and exceeded our needs, I couldn't wait to share the experience with Chris.

"Before we get into the lesson this week, Chris," I said, *"I have to tell you a story."* We sat across from each other at our usual table toward the back of the coffee shop. I told him my concerns about the CGF budget back in January, and showed him the prayer in my workbook.

"Then, God began answering my prayers," I said. *"First, Tori Kelly donated $25,000 in prize money from Celebrity Family Feud. Then, the Living Tombstone band donated $20,000, the proceeds from their Orlando concert, to CGF in honor of Christina and Marcus. And the Christina birthday-month campaign, which costs us nothing to produce, brought in $10,000."*

Chris was visibly moved. He admitted that all week he had wrestled with the stories in Week 7. *"The way the people trusted God and then watched Him provide what they needed seemed almost too tidy, too dramatic."* He was wary of anything that smacked of "name it and claim it."

But hearing how God had worked in my life, someone who had been touched by sorrow and walked through devastating loss shook Chris. *"I know you well enough to know you are not making this up,"* he said. *"And that changes how I hear these stories."*

Time and again men like Jeff and Chris would share with me, essentially, what I feel in my own heart: *"I keep hearing, but I just want more. I want to go deeper with God."* And they'd ask to be discipled. I am so honored and humbled when men come to me with that request. I value the richness that comes from the Holy Spirit working in my life through men's ministry and mentorship.

And God continually allows me to help men learn and grow in Him, even when I feel totally inadequate. He's taught me to honor Him with my life despite my shortcomings and regardless of my circumstances. I am learning to be a man who trusts Him despite the pain of losing my girls, and I believe God is using my pain to invite men into a relationship with Him that can overcome the hurt and sorrow in the world. He's been with me, step by step and shoulder-to-shoulder revealing His love for me, even through times of tragedy and heartbreak—especially through those times. I have watched Him supplant my human love with greater spiritual love, teaching me to love Him with my whole heart, mind, soul, and strength.

So many years ago, back at Bethel Church, I had sensed something deeper than just a passing thought–that I should volunteer to help with Sunday school. It was a distinct leading in my spirit, one that didn't feel like my own idea. It felt like God's. Since moving back to New Jersey to help care for Dad, I'd had a similar feeling–except that this time it was that God was nudging me out of solitude. He kept leading me to reach out, and He'd caused a simple act of obedience to flourish into ministry that was blessing men. Since the group at Jeff's house, two new groups of men's discipleship had started. I had mentored and studied with several men during my time back in New Jersey. Aidan, David, Tom, Greg, Jack, Chuck, Josh, Matt ... just thinking of their names recalls a season rich with blessing and joy.

Dad and I loved living together in our apartment in New Jersey for almost two years, but as 2024 began to draw to a close, I found myself living between two homes again, and in many ways, between two callings. For eighteen months I had lived in New Jersey, settling into a quiet two-bedroom apartment in Marlton and caring for my ninety-six-year-old father. Those days were filled with a kind of steady grace—a routine of morning coffee together, unhurried conversations, and the simple gift of presence.

And yet, beneath it all, there remained a gentle, but persistent longing to return to California. New Jersey was certainly the nostalgic home that held all the memories of my childhood, teen, and young adult life, but California was the home Tina and I made together. I longed to be back in that home, under the same roof with Marcus and Summer, and of course, with Indy and Navi, the two lovable dogs who had become part of the heartbeat of our family. And I missed the men's fellowship and ministry I'd been part of at Calvary Westlake.

At the same time, life in California was shifting for Marcus and Summer. Marcus had stepped into a new season as a tour manager with alternative rock band, TLT. He would be spending a lot more time traveling the country as their tour manager and lead guitarist. Summer had just begun her first job and was working long days that were stretching her schedule and her strength. It became clear that the house, though full of life in some seasons, would often sit quiet, and the dogs would be alone more than we had ever intended.

The natural conclusion seemed simple: I would fly out, bring the dogs back to New Jersey to live with Dad and me. It would not be easy, managing two dogs from our apartment, but it was doable. I had already imagined the routine—quick drives to open spaces for early morning walks and all that adapting life around their needs would entail to keep them happy and healthy. For a few months, from October through December, that plan felt settled.

But God has a way of interrupting our well-made plans.

One evening in December, Marcus called. As we talked, he shared something Summer had been quietly processing.

"My travel schedule stretches from May through the end of the year," he said. *"I'll be away for weeks at a time."*

Summer was beginning to realize that it wasn't just the dogs she would miss. It was the presence and companionship of other people. She wasn't sure she'd like the feeling of being alone in a large, quiet house.

"Summer's never really lived alone before," Marcus said. *"In Vietnam, she had always been surrounded by family; even her grandparents lived under the same roof."*

Aloneness, in that sense, was new to Summer.

At first, my instinct was practical.

"We could find someone to come by each day, walk the dogs, spend some time in the house," I suggested, but even as I said it, I knew a dog-walker and housekeeper wouldn't address the deeper need Summer was expressing. This wasn't just about care, it was about connection.

Marcus's next words shifted everything clearly into focus.

"Summer's asking why you and Pop can't just move here," he said.

We both knew what the answer to that had always been.

"You know Pop," I said, sighing. *"He'll say he's too old, and all his doctors are in New Jersey. And he'll ask, 'What about Carole and the rest of the family?'"*

The next day, as if divinely orchestrated, my sister Carole came to visit Dad in our apartment. We sat talking together in the living room.

"Are you two excited for the dogs to come live in New Jersey?" Carole asked. *"I am,"* she said, smiling. Our family had always loved dogs.

"We're actually rethinking all that, right now," I said. I mentioned the previous night's conversation with Marcus about Dad and me moving to California to live with him and Summer.

Carole turned to Dad and asked, almost casually, *"Would you ever consider moving to California?"*

His answer came without hesitation. *"Wherever Bud goes, I will go."*

We had never heard him say that before. Quiet. Certain. Unforced. I remember glancing at Carole and silently mouthing, *"That's new."*

I smiled. But inside, something deeper stirred. There was a calm confidence in Dad's voice that carried more than agreement, it carried trust. In that moment, the conversation shifted from possibility to direction. We began talking through what it could look like: the warmth of California's climate, the comfort of having family all around him, the practical blessing of a first-floor living space, all the comforts within easy reach. It wasn't just workable. It felt right.

The next morning, over coffee, I asked him plainly, *"Dad, would you really consider moving to California?"*

He looked at me and asked, *"Do you think I can make it?"*

He meant the travel.

"I do," I told him.

And just like that, we began to think it through.

"Driving would take eight days," I said.

"No, I wouldn't be up for that," Dad said. *"How about the train?"*

"A train would take four, with transitions along the way," I said.

When we considered the cost, the time, and the strain on Dad, flying became the clearest path. Even though it would be a six-hour flight, it seemed most manageable and direct.

Dad's cardiologist and family doctor both agreed that the move could actually benefit him. The climate, the daily presence of family, even the companionship of the dogs, all of it could contribute to his well-being, not just physically, but in spirit.

In the days that followed, I heard Dad sharing the news on the phone with family and friends; his voice was steady, even excited. At Christmas dinner, everyone began talking about visiting us in California.

The days between Christmas, 2024 and the New Year were spent intently focused on the move. What had started as a plan to relocate our dogs had become something far more meaningful. It had become a movement of love, drawing our family closer together, not farther apart.

A friend reminded me of words spoken long ago in the book of Ruth, when Ruth declares her devotion to her mother-in-law, Naomi: *"Where you go, I will go. Where you stay, I will stay."*

Albert "Bud" R. Grimmie, Sr.

Chapter Eighteen

Steady Love

What I witnessed in my father that day was more than willingness. It was loyalty. It was trust. It was love choosing to move toward relationship, toward togetherness, toward whatever came next. Trust like that didn't happen overnight; it was born of a relationship that is personal and real. It reminded me that God pursues that kind of love relationship with us. He doesn't invite us into a formula. He invites us into fellowship. He's not like a vending machine, where we put in a few spare coins, and he doles out whatever we ask. God engages us; he teaches, leads, corrects and reassures. He asks us to trust Him.

That's when I began to see my habit of morning prayer in a whole new light. It was not just a list of spiritual thoughts I'd formed over time from reading Scripture. It was a map, or better yet, a set of twelve markers God had planted across the landscape of my life. I lifted my head and let my gaze wander out the window and into the backyard. It was one of mine and Tina's favorite places to spend quiet time together. The beautiful stonework made me think of how God had built the story of my life around my need for Him. Every marker represented something He had taught me, often through struggle, often through waiting, often through pain.

Being with my father in his advancing years, watching time do what time always does, I found myself thinking not only about him, but about the long path God had carried me on. The years behind me no longer felt like scattered chapters. They began to feel connected, as though the Lord had been leaving signposts all along the road, markers I had noticed one at a time, but had never fully stood back to see together.

For years, the words of Psalm 143:8 made their way into my mornings. *"Let me hear in the morning of your steadfast love, for in you I trust. Make me know the way I should go, for to you I lift up my soul."* Sometimes I whispered them quietly over a cup of coffee before the rest of the house woke up. There were times when I prayed the words with confidence, and moments when I prayed through tears or exhaustion, just barely hanging on.

But over time, I realized that those morning prayers were becoming more than words. They were being built, like a framework giving strength and structure to my life in ways no one else could see. They were like rebar buried beneath concrete, holding it together under weight and pressure, keeping the structure from failing when it's tested, when that hidden strength matters.

Looking back now, I can see the framework God was building beneath almost every chapter of my life. I didn't recognize it every time, but throughout my life–which was not perfect or painless, nor untouched by tragedy–God was fortifying my dependence on Him.

Years before I understood *how deeply I would need God*, I thought life was mostly about trying harder to be a good person. I thought that by being decent enough I could balance the scales in my favor with God. Then Tom Horner had shared a simple Bible tract with Ephesians 2:8,9 and John 3:16. I still remember the shock of realizing salvation was not something earned, but received. I was incapable of saving myself, and God's grace felt almost too good to be true.

For the first time, I saw clearly that my behavior wasn't the problem. I needed to be rescued, much the same as my dad had from that pond. I needed life. I needed God. And once that realization entered my heart, I knew I needed more than just improved actions or religious piety; I needed a new heart.

"Create in me a clean heart, O God."

Over the years I'd learn how easy it is for fear, pride, bitterness, selfish ambition, and discouragement to quietly settle into my soul and contaminate my motives and actions. Sometimes the contamination came from the world around me, and sometimes it rose from within me. But God remained patient, renewing me again and again; sometimes through Scripture and conviction, sometimes through suffering, but always with love. I began learning what it meant that His mercies are "new every morning."

Through some of the darkest valleys of my life God has carried me, mercifully reminding me that, *"There is therefore now no condemnation for those who are in Christ Jesus."* There were moments after Christina died when grief attacked me from every direction. Lingering self-doubt and incessant questions racked my mind. Could I have done something differently? Could I have protected her? Could I have somehow changed the outcome of that night? Sorrow has a way of turning inward, if you let it, and mine convinced me that I had failed my daughter and failed God. But in time, through tears, Scripture, and prayer, God reminded me that my standing before Him was not based on my perfection or perfect actions, but on Christ's righteousness. He offered grace in place of condemnation, love instead of rejection.

And even in my grief, He kept showing me what it meant to be "more than conquerors through Him who loved us." Christianity is not about a philosophy, idea, or concept; it's about a Person. It's not simply about believing certain truths. It's about surrendering to Jesus.

"Submit yourselves therefore to God." Those words from James 4:7 resonated with me particularly in seasons where my plans changed suddenly, and when the future felt uncertain. There were times when I had to decide whether I truly trusted God, or merely trusted when the outcomes were what I preferred. In the face of moving my family to California, or making career decisions, confronting health scares and navigating financial uncertainty, or coping with loss and loneliness, I found myself posing the same question: Would I trust Him with this, too?

I learned to trust God not just when life made sense, and not only when prayers were answered the way I hoped, but in the midst of uncertainty. And somehow, over the years, through trials and triumphs, that surrender became less frightening and more freeing. The more I submitted my life to God, the more I realized that I was never carrying my burdens alone.

When I accepted that He was with me in every circumstance, I learned to *ask Him for wisdom* to make good decisions that were well-informed, but also the kind of wisdom that James describes in the Bible, wisdom from above. There were times in my life when I couldn't see ten feet ahead. Whether it was meeting Tina, raising Marcus and Christina, starting the Foundation, or the countless "coincidences" that no longer feel that way at all, God rarely showed me the whole road at once. He usually showed me just enough for the next step. Looking back now, I can see His fingerprints on so many decisions that felt uncertain in the moment we had to make them.

Some of the clearest guidance came not through dramatic signs, but through quietly walking with God day after day, *surrendering every aspect of my life to God's purposes.* I used to think that worship mostly happened in church buildings. But over time I realized worship could happen in Verizon lift trucks, hospital rooms, and airport terminals. It could happen in kitchens and funeral homes, in Bible studies, and in ordinary conversations. Worship for me became daily life, in all its imperfection, honestly surrendered to God.

For years I also thought of spiritual warfare as a symbolic language, a "church thing," that had nothing to do with everyday life. But suffering had a way of pulling back my arbitrarily erected curtain. When the lies attacked my mind and discouragement weakened my soul, when temptation was slowly eroding my hope and darkness compelled me to give up, spiritual warfare stopped being theoretical. These attacks were more than just mental. The Bible and my own lived experience confirmed that in this life there is a lot more going on than meets the eye. And yet, through all of it, God never left me defenseless. *Truth, righteousness, faith, salvation, the Word of God, and prayer were real.* The armor of God was real.

And I needed the *whole armor of God* to protect my heart, mind, and soul from forces operating in this world to destroy my faith in Him. When Christina was killed, I nearly lost myself down a black hole of deep anger. I chased conspiracy theories about her death and at first blamed myself, then God for not protecting her. But, as Tina had done so often over the years, He reminded me to read Ephesians 6:10-18, to clothe myself spiritually in the armor He'd provided to protect me and help me stand against spiritual evil rather than focus on human enemies. God sustained me in the battle and drew my heart back to right thinking about Him.

And in every season of my life, like rebar undergirding concrete and holding me together, *abiding in Christ became absolutely essential.* Apart from Him I could do nothing. There were times when I felt Scripture come alive in supernatural ways. Verses surfaced while I was driving.

Truths came to mind exactly when I needed them. Sometimes entire passages flooded my thoughts while I worked alone, high above the ground in a Verizon bucket truck. God's word became more than information. It became life. And it changed the way I looked at mine. *Jesus said He only did what He saw the Father doing.* Instead of constantly asking "What do I want to do?" I slowly began asking, *"Where is God already at work?"* I learned to see the Father working through relationships and avenues to help hurting people, through doors of opportunity quietly opening at exactly the right moment, and even through suffering.

I realized that underneath it all was His amazing, *steady love for me.* The love of God was the framework holding my life together. Suddenly I experienced the chain reaction of His love for me leading to my thankfulness that enabled me to love God with all my heart, soul, mind and strength. There were times when I felt held together by nothing more than His love. In it, even my suffering began to change shape. It did not become inherently good or painless; instead it became something God could use for His purposes.

The older I get, the more I understand what the Apostle Paul meant when he spoke about "an eternal weight of glory." This world is beautiful, but it's also broken. Our bodies weaken. People die. Hearts ache and dreams collapse. And still, somehow God keeps whispering that this is not the end of the story. *There is glory waiting on the other side of this suffering.*

Jesus said in Matthew 11:28, *"Come to Me, all who are weary and heavy-burdened, and I will give you rest."*

There were nights after Christina's death where sleep barely came, moments when my grief was palpable. Silence itself felt too heavy to bear. But beneath it all, sometimes faintly, sometimes powerfully, there remained the steady love of God. And in Him, I find rest that sustains me. Not escapism or denial, but a deep resting of my soul in the faithfulness of God. I don't have explanations for everything. My daughter was murdered. My wife was not healed this side of Heaven. *My heart is not free from sorrow and suffering. But I rest in Jesus in the midst of it all.* If there is any strength in me at all, it is only because God, in His steadfast love, kept building and reinforcing what I could not yet see.

I'm amazed that these revelations were not simply points I had developed a habit of praying through every morning. They were places where God had met me. They were truths He had written into my story, into my life. My life experiences were a journey, punctuated by markers showing me where He had found me, corrected me, and steadied me. I could look back over my life and see where He'd comforted me, loved me, and led me forward.

Morning prayer

Maybe that is part of what it means to walk with God over a lifetime. We keep thinking we are just learning isolated lessons, only to discover later that He has been building a whole testimony, weaving a story of His love in our lives. Sometimes, He lets us see at once that He's been connecting the dots all along.

After I returned to the West Coast, God kept growing the men's groups in New Jersey–five men were baptized out of our groups. Back home in Thousand Oaks, He's blessed me with the opportunity to mentor another small group of men, one of whom wants to host an Alpha program in his home.

And He's begun restoring the joy in our family home. I remember that first Thanksgiving and Christmas after Tina was gone. Marcus and I were too heartbroken to celebrate. In 2018 our family traditions remained packed away, stored in boxes full of memories too painful to open.

How different the holidays would be just seven years later. Marcus' wife, my daughter-in-law, Summer has begun to stir new life into the season like a welcome breath of fresh air. Out of her love for family and a beautiful servant's heart, she prepared her first American Thanksgiving dinner with all the trimmings. The meal and our time together was wonderful in a way the holiday hadn't been for a long time.

And at Christmas, she lovingly decorated the Christmas tree. Nearly every ornament brought back a story to share. One day, Summer might even make Grandmom Milos' baklava, with a Vietnamese twist. We gathered, thankful for each other, thankful to be together, thankful for memories of our loved ones and the start of new family traditions. The future in California looks bright for our little family—Marcus, Summer, Dad, our dogs Indy and Navi, and me.

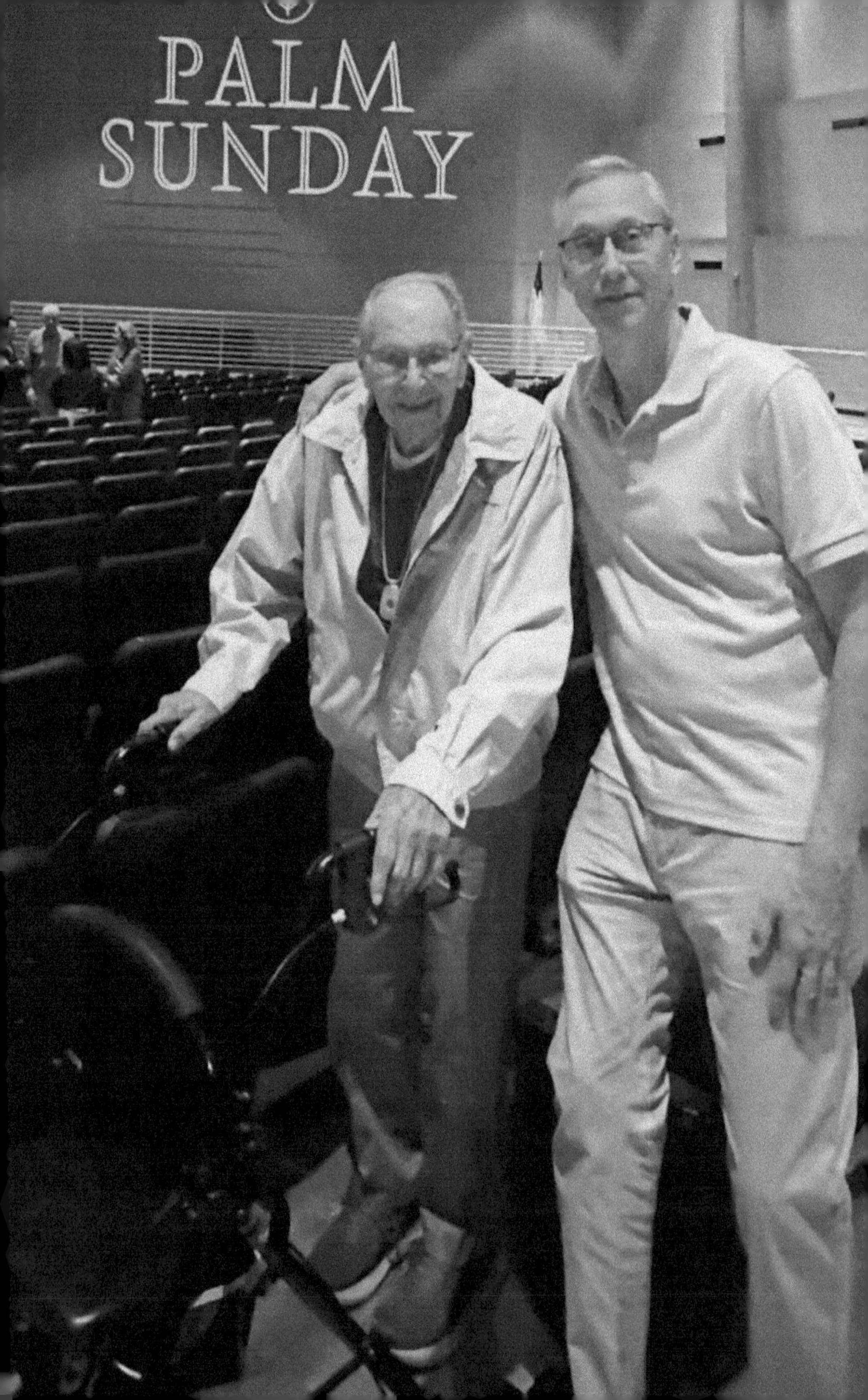
PALM
SUNDAY

Chapter Nineteen

The Father at Work

Throughout our life together Tina and I discovered lots of books and programs that helped us grow closer to God and to each other, and many that showed us ways to serve him and share his love with other people. One of our most cherished was the *Experiencing God* study by Henry Blackaby. I'd started it on my own, but when Tina's cancer returned we went through the study together. We'd work on the lessons independently during the week, then come together to review and share on Saturday.

We finished as expected on a Saturday, and on Sunday Pastor Dave Marks, a dear friend and spiritual mentor to Tina, was returning to the pulpit after being on sabbatical. That morning he preached a sermon that summed up everything we'd found so inspiring about *Experiencing God*. We were so excited and had learned so much, we'd already started praying about hosting the study for married couples in our home. We were eager to hear what Pastor Marks thought.

Tina loved Pastor Marks. He commended her often as a child of God with a heart for God and his people. It was Pastor Marks' idea to hire Tina as the school receptionist at Bethel and eventually as a member of his staff, validating her spiritual growth in a way that was precious to her. We both valued his wisdom and discernment, so were thrilled that his sermon seemed like the confirmation we needed to move ahead. But when we talked with him after service, to our surprise, he said he hadn't heard of the *Experiencing God* study.

Left: Bud Sr. and Bud Jr., Palm Sunday service, 2025

Bud and Tina saw God work in the lives of family and friends

Rather than daunted, Tina and I were even more excited and awed at how God was working in our lives. He had separately led Pastor Marks and us to the same biblical principles, which felt like the answer to our prayers. Soon after we hosted an *Experiencing God* study in our home every Saturday for twelve weeks. Tina and I often looked back on it as one of the most memorable and enriching experiences of our spiritual lives together.

Of the many principles we learned and applied from the study was practicing the habit of watching for evidence of the Father working in people's lives. John 6:44 was etched in our minds: *"No one can come to me unless the Father who sent me draws them ..."* We learned to discern him drawing people out, and we'd join in his work by sharing the Gospel and helping them begin a personal relationship with him. We had the privilege of seeing God touch many people's hearts and transform their lives, including some in our own family.

One Sunday after church Dad and I sat enjoying the peace and quiet of a sunny afternoon at home in Southern California. He leaned in, somewhat conspiratorially and confided, *"You know all those years I kept saying, 'I'm not worthy to go to Heaven. Your mother, she was worthy. Your sister, you, and Tina you're all worthy, but I'm not?'"*

Bud Sr. and Caroline, Just Married

His words often troubled my heart over the years, especially now that he was nearing one hundred.

In winter of 2009, when my mom went into hospice, before she came home for the last time, she held my hand with both of hers and looked me in the eyes.

"Please, make sure Dad and Carole both know what we know," she said. Her eyes filled with tears.

I was taken off guard, not sure what she was getting at. *"What's that mom?"* I asked, prepared to console her.

"You know—that they just have to *believe in Jesus,"* she said. *"Just make sure, make sure they know."* I can still hear the emotion in her voice. Nothing in the world mattered more to her.

"I will, Mom," I promised.

But, try as I might, most conversations with Dad about faith ended with some variation of the words he'd said: *"I'm not worthy."*

In desperation I'd hand written him a letter, hoping he would read it and that the Holy Spirit would help him understand—and convict him of the truth of the Gospel.

Dear Dad,

I've been wanting to write you a letter for some time now. Sometimes I still can't believe I'm living in California. I really love you, Pop!

I'm sure you think about Mom a lot. I do too. I sure miss her. I think about her sitting on the couch (her famous position) reading her Bible mostly every morning.

I know I've said this to you before, but I feel compelled to write to you about it so you can think about it and consider how important Mom and I believe it is.

Dad's voice interrupted my reverie.

"Now, I realize that's why Jesus came," he said. He sounded confident; excited, even. *"Because no one was really worthy. His death and resurrection make the way for us to go to Heaven."*

His words literally completed what I'd written in the letter, what Mom and I prayed Dad would come to believe and accept. I was astonished. Maybe I shouldn't have been, but I was! Now Dad believed, and we will all be together again in a place better than anyone could ever imagine.

***

As simple as that sounds, believing that God's plan is enough to give us life after death is all anyone needs to go to Heaven. But building a relationship with Jesus that withstands the suffering and sorrow that can come with this life takes work. Just like maintaining human relationships, keeping a deep, abiding connection to God requires us to invest ourselves beyond trusting his plan to keep us out of hell. Marcus' epiphany from years before, watching kids drift and fall away from the faith after the Teen Alpha program still resonates. Abiding in Christ must become a way of life, a commitment, or we drift. Old habits resurface, and our excitement for godly living fades, along with the feeling of connection and intimacy with God.

But for everyone willing to pursue intimacy with God, for anyone committed to loving Him with their whole heart He has the power and is eager to transform lives.

No one would ever believe that Tina's mom, Gina would give her heart to Jesus and become the kind of mother who could respond with love and patience to Tina in a moment of doubt, fear, anger, and distrust, but I can attest, that is exactly what happened.

I had been visiting Gina on my lunch break at the nursing home where she lived in 1989. We talked a lot about life and faith. She shared her regrets about not investing in her relationship with Tina the way she felt she should have.

Sensing God's Holy Spirit moving in her remorse, I shared the Gospel with her. *"Jesus died to pay for our sins, Gina,"* I said. *"His resurrection proved the debt was paid, and by believing we can go to Heaven."*

"That's what my Tina told me," she said.

We prayed together, and Gina accepted Jesus as her Savior.

A short while later Gina developed leukemia and was hospitalized. I had just been hired by Bell Telephone at the time, but before I could officially start I had to complete a three-week on-site training program in North Jersey. Tina and I had only been married for a little over a year, and because of her history, being apart stirred anxiety in both of us. The company put us new-hires up in a Howard Johnson motel during the week, and I drove home every weekend, counting the hours until I'd see her again.

The Bell Tel training included a grueling pole-climbing course that made for long, wearying days, but that Friday the instructor announced that if we completed our pole climbing aerial maneuvers successfully, we could stow our gear and take off early for the weekend.

Motivation hit instantly. I was one of the first to hit the pole yard, fully suited up in a long-sleeve denim jacket, heavy leather belt and safety strap, thick gloves, steel-toe boots, and the climbing hooks-gaffs strapped to my ankles. Scaling a twenty-foot utility pole supported by metal spikes driven into wood is no easy task, never mind doing it in July heat pushing ninety-five degrees and wrapped in heavy gear that trapped every ounce of sweat. But we had practiced. And home was calling.

Up I went, fast and focused. I drove in the drive hook, maneuvered around the pole, and completed the required moves. Then I pulled the drive hook free, clipped it into my belt bag, and began the treacherous descent. Descending is the part they warn you about. That's where the most falls happen. You have to drive the spikes into the wood, shifting your full weight back and forth one at a time over and over until you reach the ground. I can feel my blood pressure rise, just remembering it.

I made it down safely, stripped off my gear at the locker, stuffed everything inside, and hurried to my car. Driving home felt like victory. Week two finished, only one week left until graduation.

When I got home, Tina greeted me with that familiar excitement and warmth I loved and missed so much. We rushed through dinner and headed to the hospital to visit with Gina. We were enjoying the visit with her mom when suddenly Tina's eyes narrowed, anger flashing across her face. She pointed menacingly at my left hand.

"Where is your wedding ring?" she demanded, her voice sharp and shaking.

My stomach lurched. Stunned, I looked down at the third finger of my left hand where the ring should've been, but wasn't. My mouth opened and closed, yet no words came out. I was mystified, my brain suddenly as empty as the blank space on my finger. It didn't matter. Tina had more than enough words for both of us.

"I don't know," I finally managed to stammer.

"How can you not know?" she fumed. *"You're cheating on me! Taking off your ring when you're away from me, and ... and ..."*

Her pain poured out in waves. She cried, accused, stepped toward me, then away again. Years of fear whirling around the circle of the missing ring. Tina was just getting started, but before she reached full throttle, Gina interrupted, her voice soft but firm.

Calm and steady in the middle of Tina's storm, she said, *"Tina, you know Bud. He wouldn't do anything to hurt you, especially something like what you're thinking."*

Tina's parents, Skip and Gina, had divorced after a tumultuous dysfunctional marriage. They argued constantly over finances, with Gina often erupting in a volatile rage that sent Skip silently to his car, and often into the arms of other women. Gina lost no love over unfaithful men. I wasn't sure what to expect, but her words and demeanor surprised me.

"I'm sure there's a better explanation than that, sweetheart," she said. She motioned for Tina to come closer and patted the bed for her to sit down.

Tina, wild-eyed and frozen mid-rant, nevertheless crossed the room and sat by her mother's bedside. But not before firing off a scorching glance in my direction.

Gina patiently helped me retrace my steps to try to figure out what had happened to my wedding ring. Her forehead wrinkled, deep in thought, she looked at me and asked, *"Were you wearing gloves at school?"*

Still dazed, I nodded. *"Yeah, we only wear them when we climb poles. That was the last thing I did before leaving."*

She smiled a small, peaceful smile and nodded in satisfaction. *"That's probably where it is, then,"* she said.

God healed Gina and Tina's relationship

I glanced at Tina as relief flickered across her face, but Gina's wise words weren't enough to erase the damage already done. Tina was so hurt and confused. The rest of the weekend was strained, heavy with silence punctuated by hurtful accusations.

Monday morning I got to the training center early and made a beeline for my locker. I tore it open and dug through my gear. When my fingers slipped into the left glove and touched the ring where it lay deep inside, I nearly collapsed with relief. I found the nearest pay phone and called Tina.

It was months before she truly believed I hadn't taken my wedding ring off intentionally. It was more than a year before trust really began to settle fully between us. Looking back, that moment was part of a foundation being laid in our marriage, of learning how to stand together when fear, history, and misunderstanding collided.

Tina and I witnessed God's power to transform Gina's heart from the searing pain of betrayal in her own marriage into one gently determined to promote healing in ours. We believed in God's power to change lives, and witnessed Him do it over and over in the lives of people we knew and loved, and even in people whose hearts were united to ours in grief. When Christina died, Tina and I prayed that the excruciating pain of our grief would not overshadow the amazing impact of her life and love for Him.

***

During a writing session at Henson Studios Christina was introduced to Stephen Rezza, a producer working in a studio across the hall, and they immediately hit it off. Her manager set up some writing sessions for them to work on new song ideas. From the start Christina felt collaborating with Stephen was different than with other producers she'd worked with. He understood her musically. He clearly got it when she talked about incorporating video game sounds or music from Queen or Metallica into her pop genre.

Christina invited Tina and I to meet Stephen at Henson. His studio was awesome, in keeping with the history of the building—it was originally home to Charlie Chaplin studios, Hanna-Barbera and later, A&M Records—and the giant Kermit the Frog statue that greeted us outside.

While the ladies went to the restroom, I chatted with Stephen. He'd been asking Christina about faith, and she'd said, *"You should talk to my dad."*

"So, Christina tells me you have questions about Christianity," I began. *"She thought I might be able to help."*

He shared how he'd grown up reading the Bible and praying because of his mother. Then at seventeen he joined a garage band, writing music and touring in a van. He was transparent about being pulled away from any faith in God he might've had. I could relate considering my past in high school and the Navy.

"But talking to Christina, seeing the joy and excitement she has talking about spiritual things and Scripture makes me excited to learn," he said.

They met on April 1, and in May, Christina left to open for band *Before You Exit* on their 2016 *All The Lights Tour*, set to run for two weeks. On June 10, 2016 she was gone. In the whirlwind of two months and ten days prior to her death, Christina and Stephen completed three songs together: *Sublime*, *Invisible*, and *Steady Love.*

Christina's producer and friend, Stephen Rezza

Stephen attended Christina's funeral and memorial services, and sometime in August he called to see if we could get together to talk. He was still deeply grieving, as we all were. We met at a local Starbucks and talked. I shared the gospel with him simply and directly. He accepted Christ and later found a church to attend near his home. We've maintained a friendship, and Stephen has helped us immensely with Christina's music. He produced her posthumous album, *All Is Vanity,* that we released in 2017 on the anniversary of her death. What a joy to know that the Father still uses Christina's love for Jesus to draw her friends into relationship with Him.

Christina
Grimmie
Foundation

Chapter Twenty

The Christina Grimmie Foundation

Almost immediately after Christina was killed our family received an overwhelming outpouring of love and support from family, friends, and even complete strangers. From the two Jonathans and their families getting me to and through the airport, my sister Carole and nephew Nicky, the McDonoughs, and Brian and Mandy Teefey rushing to be with us in Florida, to Adam Levine graciously paying for Christina's funeral, and Christina's youth pastor, Jason George, who traveled the country sharing Christina's story, along with countless others who reached out to help. Their love and kindness held us up during one of the darkest times of our lives.

We are eternally grateful, and out of our gratitude Tina, Marcus, and I began thinking about how we could memorialize Christina by paying forward the kindness shown to us.

Just two days later, a mass shooting took place at The Pulse nightclub near The Plaza, where Christina performed her last concert. The incident left more than one hundred people killed or injured, and scores of family and friends of the victims devastated. Marcus had read an article reporting that almost half of the GoFundMe campaigns set up to help those people were fraudulent.

"Dad, I don't think there's anybody out there helping these people the way we've been helped after Christina," he said.

Christina Grimmie Foundation Annual Gala;
Christina and Adam Levine look on

Marcus has always had a heart for helping, not just with words, but with thoughtful and caring actions. Despite all he'd been through, his compassion for people who were hurting hadn't changed. That compassion and his love for Christina spurred him to action. He researched and found one small organization out of Philadelphia that was doing the best it could to help victims of gun violence, but they were hard-pressed to meet the overwhelming need. It occurred to Marcus that aiding the victims of The Pulse Nightclub shooting might be a way for our family to honor Christina's memory.

Officially, The Christina Grimmie Foundation was created to offer emotional and financial support to victims of gun violence and to raise funds to promote breast cancer awareness and research, but what was going on in our hearts felt much more like family and friends coming together to help people who were hurting and in need. We even tenderly call them *Green Hearts*–a term that seemed to fittingly unite us with the people we serve. It felt like what Christina had done by lovingly calling her fans/friends, "*frands*."

The first gala kicked off our fundraising efforts, and the Foundation received overwhelming support on the West Coast. Soon, we were fielding requests from people back East who also wanted to hear about what we were doing.

Tina and I started making plans to meet family and friends in New Jersey to tell them about CGF and let them know how they could lend their support. Our word-of-mouth campaign quickly took on a life of its own. Suddenly, it occurred to us that the Foundation had garnered enough momentum to warrant hosting a fundraiser on the East Coast.

CGF board members and friends, Tony Scott (deceased) and Sue Procko

On March 10, 2018 we honored Christina's memory, celebrating what would have been her 25th birthday on March 12th at The Mansion in Voorhees, NJ.

June 10, 2026 will mark a decade without Christina here on earth. To honor her life and legacy, The Christina Grimmie Foundation will host GrimmieFest, a weekend of festivities celebrating the impact she had on so many people because of her love for Jesus.

Kurt Schneider and Sam Tsui pay moving tribute to Christina

Christina Grimmie Foundation Annual Gala

My wife Tina fought a long and courageous battle with cancer, never giving up hope and choosing to let the journey make her better instead of bitter, letting her own suffering produce compassion. People often ask how we managed to keep going after Christina's death. The honest answer is that some days we hardly knew. Grief changes everything. After devastating loss life feels divided into two realities: the world before, and the world after.

And yet in the middle of that sorrow, even our grief began to change. The pain didn't disappear, instead it started moving outward through compassion. That was at the heart of beginning The Christina Grimmie Foundation.

At first, helping families affected by gun violence felt emotionally overwhelming. Every story echoed our own heartbreak. Every grieving parent felt familiar, and every shattered family prodded wounds we understood all too well. Yet something sacred was happening in those moments, too. We weren't just giving financial support. We were looking into the eyes of people living through the unimaginable and saying: *You are not alone. We understand this road.*

The Foundation did not heal us by distracting us from grief. It helped heal us by giving our grief somewhere to go. Strangely enough, some of the moments when I've felt closest to Christina since her death have come while helping hurting people in her name.

I've seen how God can redeem pain without pretending the pain itself is good. Healing is not forgetting, but for us, serving people who are experiencing what we've been through is therapeutic.

Words fail to express how much we miss Tina and Christina, but death doesn't end their story. The Christina Grimmie Foundation exists to continue their legacy of inspiration and hope.

Executive Producer Audrey Morrissey accepts CGF awards on behalf of The Voice and Adam Levine

Marcus and Tina share a tender moment

In loving tribute, my sister Carole commissioned a memorial bench and plaque honoring Christina and Tina in 2018. The bench was officially installed and dedicated on June 13, 2021 on the Ocean City Music Pier.

In loving memory of Christina Grimmie and Tina Grimmie. Forever in our hearts. Matt. 11:28 I will give you rest.

***

I think about her all the time. There was something so special about the way she made you feel like you belonged. When I first moved to LA, everything felt loud and unfamiliar. But she had this way of turning any space into home. I still remember those late nights —songs half-finished, hearts wide open. We'd laugh until we couldn't breathe, cry without saying a word. She saw people. Really saw them. And really cared. Her heart was as big as the sky. And somehow, she always knew when you needed a hug or just someone to sit with.

The Grimmie house wasn't just a place — it was a heartbeat. Spaghetti dinners, silly jokes, shared dreams — it was family. I didn't feel like the new girl in the big city anymore once she moved to town. I felt like her big sister, like someone trusted and needed. She made the world a little brighter, just by being in it. I miss her light, her laugh, her honesty. And I carry her with me, every step of the way. Anyone who knew her felt like they were the only person in the room, and no one in the world can ever take that away from her.

Note from Christina's friend, Khara

***

If I could journey back in time, I'd envelop my younger self in a comforting embrace, and tell her that she's right, that the world she knew would shift irrevocably. Nothing will ever be the same. The pain she would face would be searing, but it would not ruin her. I'd affirm that despite the heartache, the imprint Christina left would infuse her life with purpose and significance. In those moments of anguish and uncertainty, I'd remind my younger self that while the loss felt insurmountable, Christina's influence would continue to guide her, providing strength and resilience to endure the trials ahead. I'd assure her that amidst the pain, she would find a path illuminated by Christina's legacy—a life enriched by her spirit and the enduring love woven into every moment.

Letter from Christina's friend, Cassie

***

Tina and I met when she and Bud came up to Massachusetts for friends Rick and Maureen's wedding back in 1990. Bud was Rick's best man, and Tina and I really hit it off and became fast friends. It felt like I had known her forever. I could sit at her feet for hours and listen to her talk about her relationship with Jesus.

After Christina was killed, I got in the habit of texting Tina emoji hearts every day just to let her know I was there, praying for her and sending her so much love. Sometimes she would respond with a crying emoji or a broken heart. No words, just telling me how her heart was breaking. I realized that communicating this way was giving Tina an outlet to express her grief without having to put it in words if she couldn't. I was so thankful to be able to give her that. After she passed, I felt God nudging me to reach out to hurting friends in the same way I'd reached out to Tina. I've shared with a friend's brother and his wife who'd lost their son to cancer, and with another friend whose son had drowned. I'm currently sending hearts to as many as twenty-one hurting people, every day in honor of Tina and Christina. I think of it as *"Hearts for Tina."* She was such a faith-filled friend that I could share Jesus with. I truly miss and treasure that.

Taken from a letter from Tina's friend, Laurie

***

I would like to sincerely thank you for awarding me this grant. While no amount of money can ever replace my son or ease the pain of losing him to gun violence, 1 am deeply grateful for your support during this difficult time.

Your kindness, compassion, and commitment to helping families affected by gun violence mean more than words can express. Thank you for honoring my son's memory and for providing assistance that will help me move forward.

With heartfelt appreciation,

Nivia L., Green Heart

Epilogue

As I was working on this book, my dad, Albert R. Grimmie Sr. passed away on March 16, 2026. He had nearly left this life when he was just a boy of about seven years old. But for the miracle of a stranger driving by on a deserted road who, with strong hands lifted him from the dark water, he'd have been engulfed for a third and final time. A day that had begun full of sunshine and the promise of adventure had not ended in tragedy.

Years later, on a similarly beautiful day on Long Beach Island, our family looked on as a lifeguard swiftly took to the water to rescue a swimmer struggling against the pull of the current. We watched, praying that the lifeguard would reach the person in time, and then that he would be able to overcome their fearful flailing in order to save them.

Tina suddenly gasped, clutching her throat. *"That's Christina!"*

Earlier, Tina and I sat in beach chairs catching up with our dear friends, Bill and Lynn. It was one of those perfect summer days to take in the sparkling sand and the seemingly endless horizon of the Atlantic Ocean. Marcus and Christina had been body surfing in the waves with the other kids for a while when Christina came running out of the water, rubbing her eye. *"Something's in it,"* she shouted, hurrying past us and up to the beach house, just steps from the ocean. *"I'm going inside to rinse it out."*

We watched her climb onto the porch and go back into the house then went back to talking, assuming she'd be back in a few minutes. The piercing sound of a lifeguard's whistle jolted us out of our conversation, and we turned as he sprinted past our blanket, still blowing the whistle, eyes focused on the water. Without hesitation, he charged into the surf and dove into the waves.

After rinsing her eye, Christina had run back from the beach house and slipped unnoticed into the waves from a spot away from our group. The current had caught her almost immediately and was pulling her out, fast. We watched, horrified as she tried to swim sideways toward the other kids, but the tide was stronger than she was. To make matters worse, when the lifeguard reached her, Christina initially panicked and tried to fight him off. Frightened and disoriented, to her he looked like a stranger trying to grab her. Thankfully, he managed to calm her down enough for her to hear him. *"I'm here to help you. I'm bringing you back."*

We all stood frozen at the edge of the water, much as my dad recalls his sisters doing as he was rescued from drowning in the pond. Holding our breath, we watched as the lifeguard emerged from the surf with Christina, shaken, but safe.

I posed the question earlier, and over the course of my life I have come to believe that none of us are here by chance. We are each God-ordained miracles, born with a purpose designed by Him. Our lives are not just a scattered series of random events–and neither are our deaths.

Who knows whether those harrowing brushes with death were a foreshadowing of the great rescue to come? The moment of revelation, when everything came into focus for Dad, and Tina, and Christina. The moment when, for every believer in Jesus, what once felt disconnected will suddenly make sense in the light of something far greater. The moment we are face-to-face with the Creator of the universe, who has loved us and carried us every step of the way.

As Dad's and Tina's physical bodies failed, and Christina opened her arms to the unimaginable, the Savior miraculously lifted them from the fog of this life and into His glorious presence in Heaven. The thought steadies me. It doesn't erase the pain of loss, but it reframes it. I'm reminded that this life, as real as it is, is not the final chapter. There are better shores ahead; a home that God himself has prepared. And keeping our eyes on that shore through this life, glimpsing it even faintly will give us the strength to keep swimming, the courage to keep going until the strong arms of the One whose steady love sustains us fulfills the longing of every heart.

About the Author

Albert R. "Bud" Grimmie is the father of the late singer Christina Grimmie. He lives in Thousand Oaks with his son, musician Marcus Grimmie, daughter-in-law Summer, and their two dogs, Indy and Navi. Bud is also the CEO and co-founder of the Christina Grimmie Foundation. He was married for 31 years to his beloved wife, Tina, who passed away from breast cancer in 2018. *Steady Love: What Every Heart Longs For* is his first publication. A portion of the proceeds from the sale of each book supports the ongoing work of the Christina Grimmie Foundation. For more Steady Love content, scan the QR code, or visit SteadyLoveBook.com.

The Christina Grimmie Foundation is a 501(c)(3) charity created to provide tangible support and services to families who have lost a loved one to gun violence, helping them begin rebuilding their lives and focus on healing rather than financial burdens or household responsibilities. Our mission is to honor the victims while supporting their families through the difficult aftermath of tragedy.

Through community support, donations, fundraising events, and direct outreach the Foundation works closely with families to provide meaningful services and a compassionate support system. When families face unimaginable loss, we meet them with love and a genuine pathway to hope. For more, visit ChristinaGrimmieFoundation.org or scan the QR code to donate.

www.ingramcontent.com/pod-product-compliance
Lightning Source LLC
LaVergne TN
LVHW052339100826
845147LV00021B/1124

* 9 7 9 8 9 9 6 0 8 4 7 1 5 *